# How To
# Soar Like An Eagle

## If you have the strength to dream, then you can soar.

Pastor Susan DeRienzo

PRESS

*How To Soar Like An Eagle*
*If you have the strength to dream, then you can soar.*
by Pastor Susan DeRienzo

Printed in the United States of America

ISBN 9781609571191

Unless otherwise indicated, Bible quotations are taken from The Holy Bible, King James Version; The Amplified Bible Parallel Edition. Copyright © 1995 by Zondervan, Grand Rapids, Michigan 49530, U.S.A.; and The Amplified Bible. Copyright © 1954, 1958, 1962, 1964, 1965, 1987 by The Lockman Foundation.

www.xulonpress.com

# Acknowledgement

❧❦❧

I dedicate the writing of this book to my family and closest friends whose loyalty, encouragement, and commitment to prayer made it possible for me to complete this book.

Abraham DeRienzo, my wonderful husband, prayer partner, and closest friend who supported me through the writing of this book.

David Jarres, the best son a mother could ever hope and pray for, gave me the King James Version /Amplified Bible Parallel Edition used for all scriptures contained in this book.

Samantha Tetro, founder and director of Samantha's Lil' Bit of Heaven, New York, for her obedience to God in anointing my head with oil and praying for God's favor and victory over death from cancer. Not given more than ten hours to live, sixteen years later, I am cancer free and in full-time ministry with my husband. To Samantha, her staff, and the family of Samantha's Lil' Bit of Heaven, I truly thank you for your prayers and devotion to God.

Patricia Marotta, a long time close friend and a great example of one who continually walks with Jesus day by day, step by step, and moment by moment. Patricia is a beacon of light who enthusiastically and continually prays for my family, our church ministry, and God's will for this book.

Virginia Sumrall, a dear friend and truly devoted prayer worrier for Jesus Christ, who fervently and continually prays with me through every challenge in my personal life and in the writing of this book.

Sara Higginbotham recognized as "The Walking Bible", daily quotes scripture feeding God's children. She is a beautiful intelligent woman of God rooted in God's Word from childhood by her mother, Ethel Albright. She graciously offered to proofread this book with her wonderful husband, Gary. Truly, there are numerous scriptures to behold in this book.

The greatest acknowledgement goes to God for blessing me with the wisdom, knowledge, and understanding necessary for the writing of this book.

# In Memory Of

My mother, Elba Medina,
Whom God used to teach the art of
Real forgiveness.

AND

My friend, Ethel Albright,
A beacon of light and everlasting
Inspiration in my life.

GOD BLESS YOU!

# *How To*
# Soar Like An Eagle

## Is Presented

To: _____

By: _____

Comments:
_____
_____
_____
_____
_____
_____
_____
_____
_____
_____

# Table of Contents

*Chapter 1*

# Who You Are In Christ

❦

In Christ Jesus, you are brave, fearless, fighting warriors, valiant heroes and champions, men and women of courage who bear arms within and throughout the Word of God. In Christ Jesus, you are favored; you have connections and influence within the body of Christ. This is possible by living a committed life unto your Lord God Almighty, the Holy One and Redeemer for all. Christ Jesus is the All Merciful, All Powerful, and All Knowing Light unto the world. When you allow yourself to be given over to Christ Jesus as your Redeemer and Lord, you become a joint heir with him; therefore enabling you to receive your inheritance from God. Acts 17:28 says that you are God's offspring. *"For in him we live, and move, and have our being; for we are also his offspring."* You, as a true believer, are entitled to every promise in God's Word through Jesus Christ. Jesus Christ is God Incarnate, the Morning Star, and the Word made flesh, your Counselor, Mediator, Advocate, and Intercessor. He is your Judge, and Great Physician, your Healer and Comforter, the Crucified Lamb of God, and true Bread of Life in whom all things are possible.

In today's world where everything is done with urgency, you easily become worn out. You find yourself so entangled in daily living that motivation to focus on God seems impossible. Family issues, financial struggles, medical conditions, and concerns for others are just a few diversions. Then there are outward influences such as television, the newspaper, politics, the stock market, the economy, homelessness, widows, orphans, the elderly, the rich, the poor, the insane, criminal acts, music, sports, drama, the list is endless. Your eyes and ears overwhelm your mind with input like a computer on overload. What do we do to fix a computer overload? We delete data. We clean house and get rid of programs or files no longer needed to make room for more important information to be stored in its memory. In addition, the computer's memory must be protected from bugs and viruses the bad stuff causing corruption. The mind is not much different from a computer and needs continued maintenance. You need to let go of your past and look at the present. Today has enough in itself to deal with. You need to sift out what doesn't belong and move on. Negative influences to the brain will cause the mind to respond in a similar way a computer reacts when given a virus. What you allow into your mind directly reflects your actions, personality, and character. Therefore, guard your mind. The world is full of haste, excitement, cruelty, and confusion. It is just like Satan, the ruler of this world, to consume your mind in an attempt to delay or put a stop to God's will for your life. How can you receive from God and live a life in Christ if you spend your time, energy, and effort on other matters? Worldly influences and outward circumstances directly reflect into your personal life. Where do you draw the line? You need to draw a boundary line in order to live a true and balanced life in Christ. He longs to hear from you daily. So, push away worldly influences, resist temptation, and give over to God those things, which would distract you from quality time with him. You must limit how much you absorb of the world and the circumstances of others in order to find a healthy balance for peace and rest in your life. You must set up camp with Jesus Christ and give more over to him in prayer. Give God more of an opportunity to reveal himself to you. He loves you and believes in you.

It is very crucial to put all your cares into Jesus' hands. He understands your concern for others. You are his child whom he deeply cares for. Jesus is fully aware of your burdens and wants to help you through them. 1 Peter 5:7 tells you to cast *"all your care upon him; for he careth for you."* When you become full of care, you worry. When you worry, you disobey God's Word by not placing your trust and care of others in him completely. 1 Corinthians 13:13 explain that love is God's greatest gift to you. Some Bible translations replace the word love with charity, meaning that love and charity are both one in the same; unconditional, self-sacri-ficing benevolence toward others. God's Word explains this even further in John 15:5-10, *"If ye abide in me, and my words abide in you, ye shall ask what ye will, and it shall be done unto you. Herein is my Father glorified, that ye bear much fruit; so shall ye be my disciples. As the Father hath loved me, so have I loved you: continue ye in my love. If ye keep my commandments, ye shall abide in my love; even as I have kept my Father's commandments, and abide in his love."* Verses 13-14 of the same chapter say, *"Greater love hath no man than this that a man lay down his life for his friends. Ye are my friends, if you do whatsoever I command you."* God will always cause you to triumph and succeed when you listen and obey him. He cares so much for you that he wants you to have it all, good health, a stable family life, and prosperity. Just keep in mind that his main priority is your relationship with him. God desires that whatever your hands touch would prosper, whatever your mind conceives of, in him, will come to pass, and that your lips would speak edification into the lives of others. Therein, lay the blessings of God's great love for you.

God demonstrates his love to all humanity in John 3:16-17, *"For God so loved the world that he gave his only begotten Son, that whosoever believeth in him should not perish, but have everlasting life. For God sent not his Son into the world to condemn the world; but that the world through him might be saved."* Therefore, love one another in

Christ as Christ loves you. The greatest gift of love offered to all humanity is the gift of Salvation through Jesus Christ. He gave you a second chance a new beginning and life for those who choose to receive it. This is how much God cares and loves you. He knows your every need and your heart's desire. However, he requires that you spend more time in communion with him. Make God top priority in your life. Make God a priority over others, television, work, your children, home life, and all things. You can do this by incorporating him into every aspect of your daily living. Focus is the key to staying in his presence. Just a few years ago a woman was asked, "How could you possibly spend all day with God when you have so much work to do?" Her response was something like this, "When I open my eyes in the morning, I say, Lord, help me to see through your understanding. As I dress, I say, Lord, cloth me in righteousness today. When I eat, I pray, Lord fill me with the meat of your Word. When I wash, I pray that God would refresh my mind, body, and soul. As I clean my house, I pray that God would cleanse me from all unrighteousness. As I work, I pray asking God for strength equal to the tasks of my day. As I am busy with my children and with others, I look up to my heavenly Father who knows all my needs before I ask him." The point is that no matter how busy you are you need to continually focus your mind on Christ; making him your *number one* priority. You must *"pray without ceasing"* 1 Thessalonians 5:17. In order for God to help you, he needs an open door of communication with you. Give all your concerns over to God. Continually trusting him with your prayers and remember to thank him for all he does for you. Give to God and he will give to you. His hand is always reaching out to you. Will you stretch out your hand toward God today? Receive from God *"and the peace of God, which passeth all understanding, shall keep your heart and mind through Jesus Christ."* Philippians 4:7.

*"Trust in the Lord with all thine heart; and lean not on your own understanding."* Proverbs 3:5. *"Be careful for nothing; but in everything by prayer and supplication with thanksgiving let your request be made known to God."* Philippians 4:6. *"Now faith is the substance of things hoped for, the evidence of things not seen."* Hebrews 11:1. Trust, devotion, and faith are the elements needed for a promise assured to you from God. Just step out in faith giving to God the circumstances that were never really yours to bear. Do not depend on your limited knowledge or understanding for resolution to a problem. Rather, trust God and have faith I him. You as a believer know that you must take God at His Word and believe by faith. Jesus said in Mark 9:23, *"If thou canst believe, all things are possible to him that believeth."* Hebrews 10:23 says, *"Let us hold fast the profession of our faith without wavering."* Psalms 37:5 says, *"Commit thy way unto the Lord; trust also in him; and he shall bring it to pass."* Bring the load you carry to God. Trust and rely on him to see you through. God tells you that by enforcing your

will over to him he will bring to pass what you ask for if you believe through unwavering committed faith and total belief in him. To have unwavering faith and remain in it, you need the full armor of God.

God through his eyes of love sees you as a soldier, a brave fighting worrier, a conqueror against all injustice and unrighteousness, an over comer and victorious in all things through him. However, you must first put on the whole armor of God to stand against the forces of darkness in this world. If you are not armed then fear, worry, money, health, family, jobs, the media, and associating with unbelievers are just a few diversions and traps Satan uses to prevent you from receiving your blessings and from having a rich rewarding relationship with Jesus Christ. When you are not wearing your suit of armor you leave yourself exposed to the blinding trap of having spent all your time, effort, and energy on the things of this world. God supplies his children with all the armor needed to stand against the strategies and deceits of Satan. You are not wrestling against flesh and blood but against the spirits of world rulers in this present darkness, against the spirit forces of wickedness.

Ephesians 6:11-18 says, *"Put on the whole armour of God that ye may be able to stand against the wiles of the devil. For we wrestle not against flesh and blood, but against principalities, against powers, against the rulers of the darkness of this world, against spiritual wickedness in high places. Wherefore take upon you the whole armour of God that ye may be able to withstand in the evil day, and having done all, to stand. Stand therefore, having your loins gird about with truth, and having on the breastplate of righteousness; and your feet shod with the preparation of the gospel of peace; above all, taking the shield of faith wherewith ye shall be able to quench all the fiery darts of the wicked. And take the helmet of salvation, and the sword of the Spirit, which is the Word of God: Praying always with all prayer and supplication in the Spirit, and watching thereunto with all perseverance and supplication for all saints."*

Having girded your loins with truth is to surround yourself with the straightforward authentic Word of God. Stay away from those who confuse and misinterpret God's Word. His Word maintains integrity, sincerity, honesty, and uprightness.

Having the breastplate of righteousness means having the spirit of Christ living in you at all times. Not being righteous in yourself but in Christ. The breastplate of righteousness is there for your protection. You are to put on the clothes of holiness, faithfulness, purity, honor, and Godliness to protect yourself and to ward off the forces of unrighteousness.

Having your feet shod with the preparation of the Gospel of Peace is to educate you in the scriptures. You must gain background, training, and experience in God's Word. God commands that all believers study His Word. *"Study to show thyself approved unto God, a workman that needeth not be ashamed, rightly dividing the Word of truth."* 2 Timothy

2:15. *O give light to them that sit in darkness and in the shadow of death, to guide our feet into the way of peace."* Luke 1:79.

Taking up the Shield of Faith means that you have chosen to take hold of your faith in God and in His Word to use as your protector against the forces of darkness. Ephesians 6:16 tells us that above all other armor you are to take up the shield of faith in order to put out the fiery darts of the wicked. Faith is expectation that takes dedication and endurance to stand against doubt. By faith, you are to expect the manifestation of God's Word. Faith honors God and God honors faith.

Having the Helmet of Salvation means to keep your mind (*helmet*) focused on the Word of God. Your mind must be redeemed back to God. You physically and mentally must release your old habits, patterns, and thought processes. This cleansing process clears and restores the mind to having the mind of Christ rather than self. Colossians 3:2 tells you to *"set your affections* [mind] *on things above, not on things of earth."* Jesus tells Nicodemus in John 3:6, *"that which is born of the flesh is flesh; and that which is born of the spirit is spirit."* You must transform your mind from the natural to the supernatural; think outside the box. God is a God of the supernatural.

Taking up the Sword of the Spirit means that believers are to engage in spiritual warfare and the struggles of life with a firm driving force of courage and fearlessness using

God's principals. Be steadfast and true to him through Jesus Christ your Lord and Savior.

For the believer life is a constant spiritual warfare against assaults from your enemies toward your soul. Spiritual courage and strength are necessary for spiritual warfare. It is by faith in God and through your Christian walk that you can combat your enemies. By faith, you choose to put on the whole armor of God and stand your ground against all that opposes God.

Notice that God did not provide armor for your back. This is because you are not to turn your back toward your enemy. You are to confront and resist your enemy who will eventually flee. Seven years ago a co-worker employed in the same department as I, would outwardly ridicule God, the things of God, and me for bearing witness of God. Many times, Lisa would tell lies about me to our boss with the hopes of getting me fired. This was very trying and mentally draining for me. I continually had to defend myself for things I would not dream of doing. I stood tall and confident in the truth around those who did not know what to believe. As stressful as my job became, I stayed in prayer and supplication with God believing that he was in control of the situation. I kept repeating that I am victorious in Christ Jesus and that the battle was his not mine. I was the instrument God chose to use to give another opportunity for salvation to one of his creations. Almost a year later and frustrated over not getting her way, Lisa finally gave up and put in for a transfer. The spirit of Satan cannot handle being around the spirit of God. God had the victory and the enemy fled to another building in a town far away. From that day on, I worked in peace and continued to bear witness to adults and children with special needs. Just remember the whole armor of God is not complete without continual fervent prayer. This means that you are to pray audibly, silently, at work, and under any circumstance with perseverance and supplication for yourself and for other believers for as long as you live in this world. God has your back if you let him.

My brothers and sisters in Christ it is by the spiritual renewing of your mind that you are able to live a life of devotion to God. His peace, mercy, and favor are yours through Jesus Christ, your Lord and Savior. All who are fully persuaded of these truths and willing to defend them are soldiers in the army of God brave, fearless, fighting worriers, valiant heroes, and champions. God created you in his image. You are a champion. With God, you are more than able to fulfill your destiny. God does not look at your past or your faults. His image of you today is what he sees through his eyes, not yours. You are special, you have God's anointing, and you have power in Jesus Christ. *"You shall know the truth and the truth shall set you free."* John 8:32.

## Chapter 2

# God's Purpose for Your Life

※❦❧❦※

Jesus gathered his disciples and spoke to them of another kingdom, a kingdom not of this world. Believed by his followers to be the Messiah and the founder of Christianity, Jesus, the Son of God, left his eternal home of bliss, angels, and divinity to enter a realm of mortal existence. The deep passion Jesus has for you is one where he willfully longs to do everything possible to heal the oppressed and bring Salvation to the world. His first disciples were; Andrew and his brother Simon called Peter, who both are from Galilee, and James and his brother John, who were mending their nets with their father Zebedee when Jesus called them. Jesus went with his first four disciples into Capernaum. He taught in the synagogue and healed a man of an unclean spirit. From Capernaum Jesus went into a desert place. Many gathered there to hear his teachings. The news of Jesus Christ continued to spread. One day while walking by the seaside

Jesus saw a man named Levi. Jesus asked Levi to follow him making Levi the fifth disciple of Jesus Christ. Great multitudes followed Jesus wanting to hear him speak and to witness healing in their lives. They wanted to receive their blessings from God through Jesus Christ. The pressing of the multitudes upon Jesus led him to instruct his five disciples, along with several others, to go up into a mountain where Jesus would meet with them shortly. It was on that mountain that Jesus Christ of Nazareth chose twelve men to train and work with him. The twelve men were, Simon Peter, James and his brother John, Andrew, Philip, Bartholomew, Matthew *(Levi)*, Thomas, James the son of Alphaeus, Thaddaeus, Simon the Canaanite, and Judas Iscariot who would betray Jesus. These men became Jesus' disciples and continued to learn while with Jesus. The disciples were privileged to much more than the multitudes. They witnessed Jesus calming the sea and walking on water, the understanding of parables, and some witnessed the transfiguration. *"And he turned him unto the disciples, and said privately, Blessed are the eyes which see the things ye see; for I tell you, that many prophets and kings have desired to see those things which ye see, and have not seen them; and to hear these things which ye hear, and have not heard them."* Luke 10:23-24.

When Jesus knew the time was right he called his twelve disciples to himself sending them out two by two to preach the message of Salvation. Jesus also gave them authority over unclean spirits and power to heal all diseases. Jesus instructed them, *"Take nothing for your journey, and whatever house ye enter into, there abide, and thence depart. And whosoever will not receive you, when ye go out of that city, shake off the very dust from your feet for a testimony against them. And they departed, and went through the towns, preaching the gospel, and healing everywhere."* Luke 9:3-6. The twelve disciples cast out many devils and anointed with oil those who were sick, and healed them. Now even greater multitudes followed Jesus and saw great miracles performed by his disciples. Therefore, Jesus chose seventy others and sent them out two by two saying to them, *"...the harvest truly is great, but the laborers are few...Behold, I send you forth as lambs among wolves."* Luke 10:2-3. Jesus instructed the seventy chosen and sent them out two by two. They returned with greater joy saying that even the devils are subject to them in his name. Jesus said, *"Behold I give unto you power to tread on serpents and scorpions, and over all the power of the enemy, and nothing shall by any means hurt you."* Luke 10:19. Just then, a lawyer stood up from among the crowd. Wanting to tempt Jesus, he asked what he should do to inherit eternal life. Jesus asked him, "What is written in the law?" The lawyer responded, "Love thy neighbor as thyself." Questioning Jesus further the lawyer asked, "Who are my neighbors?" Since the lawyer was thinking in the natural, Jesus replied with the story of the Good Samaritan in Luke 10:30-37. The scriptures explain that a certain Jewish man coming from Jerusalem fell among thieves who robbed and beat him, leaving him for dead. A priest came and passed him on the other side of the road. A Levite came, looked at the man lying in the read, and passed him on the other side of the read. Then a Samaritan, an enemy of the Jews, came saw the man and had compassion for him. The Samaritan bound his wounds placed the man on his own beast, possibly a donkey, brought him to an inn and took care of him. The next day the Samaritan left the innkeeper two pence for the expenses and said that he would pay for any additional expenses. The lawyer listening to Jesus said that the person who showed mercy is his neighbor. Jesus then told the lawyer to go and do likewise to others.

Jesus came for the Jews the lost sheep of the house of Israel. Yet his reply to the lawyer is an example of the love of God for all humanity. Another example is that of the Syrophoenician woman, a Canaanite, who is an outcast and considered unclean. She was pleading to Jesus for mercy toward her demon-possessed daughter. Jesus replied, *"I am not sent but unto the lost sheep of the house of Israel."* Then Jesus wanting to show those present the greatness of her faith said to her, *"it is not meet to take the children's bread, and to cast it to dogs."* The Syrophoenician woman said, *"Even the dogs eat the crumbs that fall from their masters table."* Jesus then healed the Syrophoenician woman's daughter because of the greatness of her faith in him. This example of God's mercy is in Mark 8:22-28. What Jesus did for this woman, he longs to do for all who receive and believe in him.

Jesus chose Peter, James, and John to go to a high mountain a place of solitude. It was there that Jesus transfigured himself before these men. Jesus revealed himself in a mountain to Peter, James, and John as God revealed himself in a mountain to Moses. Those who choose to have a deep relationship with God must withdraw from the world to a place of solitude; a quiet area where communication can peacefully and uninterruptedly take place. For Peter, James, and John this quiet moment of glory with Jesus would help to prepare them for their witness of the agony Jesus would bare in the near future. Jesus standing before them in the flesh and in all humility transformed to reveal God's power and glory. Jesus' face shined like the sun emanating strength and power. His body, filled with glory, enlightened his raiment white as light. Moses and Elijah also appeared talking with Jesus; three witnesses from Earth, three witnesses from Heaven. The three glorified saints bore witness of a glorified life after physical death. Why did Moses and Elijah appear with Jesus before the disciples? Because the Jewish nation have great respect for them even after their death; Moses representing God's promise and deliverance, Elijah representing the need for repentance leading to forgiveness. When the disciples heard Moses and Elijah talking with Jesus and longing to dwell in this glorious moment a little longer, Peter asked to build three tabernacles one for each saint to continue their communion among each other. Jesus gave no response. Then suddenly Jesus appeared alone with his disciples while God appeared in the form of a bright cloud saying, *"This is my beloved Son in whom I am well pleased, listen to Him."* Matthew 3:17. These are the same words spoken by God during Jesus' baptism by John the Baptist. In fear and trembling, the disciples fell to the ground on their faces. Jesus leaned forward gently touching them and filling them with his peace and love as he said to them, *"arise, and be not afraid."* As the disciples rose, they saw only Jesus and fear left them. Jesus appeared unto them just as before. *"And as they came down from the mountain, Jesus charged them, saying, 'Tell the vision to no man, until the Son of man be risen again from the dead,'"* Matthew 17:1-9. Jesus continued his ministry preaching God's love and that the way to the Father is through the Son. Jesus told the disciples of his death, his resurrection, and to be ready for his return. Jesus said in John 11:25, *"I am the resurrection, and the life: he that believeth in me, though he were dead, yet shall he live: and whosoever liveth and believeth in me shall never die. Believeth though this?"* When Jesus resurrected from the grave he appeared first to Mary Magdalene then to the other women returning from the grave. He also appeared before Peter, the Emmaus disciples, the seven by the sea, Steven the first martyr, Paul on his way to Damascus, to over five hundred brethren, and to the eleven disciples. When Jesus saw the eleven disciples, he stayed with them and encouraged them saying that all authority has been given to him in Heaven and of Earth.

Thus far, you know that Jesus started his ministry with four disciples, then Levi, who was Matthew, making five. Jesus later chose twelve disciples to preach repentance. He gave them authority to cast out demons, heal the sick, and sent them out two by two. As the multitude of followers grew and the needs increased Jesus chose seventy others to go out two by two to preach repentance. He also gave them authority to cast out demons and to heal the sick. They came back rejoicing over the miracles they performed through Jesus Christ. Jesus fore knew that upon his death the veil in the temple would be broken, Matthew 27:51, Mark 15:38, and Luke 23:45. There would be no more separation between Jews and Gentiles. The Jews and the Gentiles received the same Salvation. *"That the blessing of Abraham might come on the Gentiles through Jesus Christ; that we might receive the promise of the Spirit through faith."* Galatians 3:14. The telling of the parables of the Good Samaritan and the healing of the Canaanite woman's daughter are examples of God's great mercy to all. The Good Samaritan and the Canaanite woman were enemies of God because they were not Jewish. These women's faith was great. They accepted Jesus Christ as there Lord and Savior. Upon the death and resurrection of Jesus Christ, all things became new. Where you once lived by the Law of Moses, you now live by the grace and mercy of Jesus Christ. Jesus Christ of Nazareth has all authority in Heaven and on Earth. Now as Jesus leaves the Earth, ascending to heaven, he instructs his disciples to make disciples of all nations. This means you and me. *"All power is given unto me in heaven and in earth. Go ye therefore, and teach all nations, baptizing them in the name of the Father, and of the Son, and of the Holy Ghost: teaching them to observe all things whatsoever I have commanded you: and lo I am with you always, even unto the end of the world."* Matthew 28:18-20.

After Jesus death and resurrection, he met with the eleven disciples, ate and drank with them, and then commissioned them to go into all the world and teach the gospel making disciples of all nations. First, this tells you that the gospel was no longer strictly for the Jews the lost sheep of the house of Israel. When Jesus died for the sins of all humanity this included the Gentiles, the Samaritans. Jesus took upon himself the sins of every human being on the face of the earth. He brought our sins to Hell left them there and resurrected on the third day setting humanity free of guilt, shame, and all forms of sin with the exception of blasphemy. By not choosing Jesus Christ as your Lord and Savior, you exclude yourself from the Gospel of Peace. Second, Jesus commissioned the eleven disciples to make disciples of all nations through baptism and the teachings of the Gospel. Third, disciples exist from generation to generation through the acceptance of Jesus Christ, God's Word, and by being water baptized in the name of the Father, the Son, and the Holy Spirit. Baptism is a sacred oath between the believer and Jesus Christ himself. A sacred oath where you as a believer consent to a covenant relationship with God the Father, God the Son, and God the Holy Spirit. In taking this oath, the believer renounces the devil, resists temptation, and gives up one's self to the will of God. Therefore, you become free agents from this world unto Christ Jesus observing all things that Christ commands. Allow God appointed spirit-filled teachers to train you up in the knowledge of the gospel. Remember, Jesus taught the twelve disciples before they began their ministry. In addition, you have God's favor always and to the end of age. Jesus said, *"I am with you always."* In the Spirit Jesus is with all those who truly receive him. Jesus said that he would never leave you nor forsake you. After his resurrection, Jesus called his eleven disciples to the great commission, that all nations would spread the gospel through the disciplining of all humanity. The book of Acts chapter 10 tells the story of how Peter learned that God does not show partiality to anyone. Jesus wants all believers to become disciples for him those who are willing to fulfill the call of God upon their lives to live and work together to set the captives free.

All of us have gifts, talents, and abilities. The use of them aids in bringing forth the Gospel. Today we have Christ-centered schools, organizations, missionaries, retreat centers, adult homes, authors, publishers, actors, musicians, doctors, caregivers, and more because of the many believers who chose to fulfill the call of God upon their lives. Believers everywhere are working to fulfill God's great commission.

Are you? Jesus Christ wants to spread his Gospel and the knowledge of his kingdom through you a true believer in him. He wants to use all those who are willing to live and work for his glory. God created you to serve him. Your body is his temple, which houses your soul where the Holy Spirit dwells. As disciples and victors in Christ, *"Ye are of God, little children, and have overcome them; because greater is he that is in you, than he that is in the world."* 1 John 4:4 *"But the very hairs of your head are all numbered. Fear ye not therefore, ye are of more value than many sparrows. Whosoever therefore shall confess me before men, him will I confess also before my Father which is in heaven."* Matthew 10:30-32. *"Go ye into all the world, and preach the gospel to every creature."* Mark 16:15.

*Chapter 3*

# Characteristics of a Disciple

✦✦✦

"Disciple" comes from the root word "discipline." This is a difficult word to digest since most of us do not like to be disciplined. Jesus said, *"If any man comes after me, let him deny himself, and take up his cross daily, and follow me."* To take up your cross means to die to self. A sacrifice must be made to be a disciple, a follower of Jesus. Have you ever wondered why God put you on this earth? For what purpose were you created? Do you desire Jesus above anything in life, a career or personal happiness? To follow Jesus means to walk, think, and act as Jesus did, to have a deep desire to want to carry your cross for the sake of the Gospel and kingdom of heaven. This does not mean to be poor and do without. This does not mean that you have to convert anyone. As truly devoted men and women of God it is not your responsibility to convince anyone of the kingdom of God, the miracle working power of God, or of his Salvation message through Jesus Christ. It is your responsibility to preach the gospel of truth and leave the converting to God, his Son, and by his Holy Spirit. *"Not by might, nor by power, but by my spirit saith the Lord of hosts."* Zechariah 4:6. The acceptance of Christ, the manifestation of miracles, and sustaining a life in Christ Jesus comes through unwavering faith and continual prayer. Salvation comes from letting go, surrendering all to God the Father, God the Son, and God the Holy Spirit. Discipleship works the same way. You must surrender unto God your will and desire to convert another person no matter how close you are to that person. Moreover, I am talking about a deep yearning for Christ above all else, believing that Christ is the center of true happiness and fulfillment by his divine standards and not the world's standards. As in Romans 12:1, *"I Beseech you therefore, brethren, by the mercies of God, that ye present your bodies a living sacrifice, holy, acceptable unto God, which is your reasonable service."* True discipleship requires obedience and sacrifice. To be a true disciple of Jesus Christ means to take up your cross daily for the sake of his will, not yours.

**Some important characteristics that disciples have:**

1. Disciples bear fruit.
2. Disciples persevere.
3. Disciples demonstrate the love of God.

4. Disciples bear the cross of Jesus.

5. Disciples forsake self to abide in Christ Jesus.

<u>Disciples bear fruit:</u> In John chapter 14 Jesus is speaking to his disciples at the last supper saying that he would be with them just a little longer. Jesus comforts his disciples by saying, *"Verily, verily, I say into you, he that believeth in me,* [meaning all people from generation to generation, not just those present in the room with him] *the works that I do shall he do also; and greater works than these shall he do; because I go unto my Father."* John 14:12. Jesus is telling his disciples that he will be leaving soon but that his great work, miracles, and gifts will continue through his disciples and all those who truly live a life through him. *"And whatsoever ye shall ask in my name, that will I do, that the Father may be glorified in the Son. If ye ask any thing in my name, I will do it. If ye love me, keep my commandments."* John 14:13-15. *"If ye abide in me and my words abide in you, ye shall ask what ever ye will, and it shall be done unto you. Herein is My Father glorified, that ye bear much fruit; and so shall ye be my disciples."* John 15:7-8.

<u>Disciples persevere:</u> Jesus requires that you run with endurance the race that is set before you keeping your eyes on him. He who himself endured the cross for the sake of the joy of salvation sets the example for all believers that you may not grow weary and lose heart. Jesus endured tremendous hostility, pain, and adversity for your sake. Jesus

requires you to do the same toward the building up of the body of Christ. *"For God hath not given us the spirit of fear; but of power, and of love, and of a sound mind. Be not now therefore ashamed of the testimony of our Lord, nor of me his prisoner: but be thou partaker of the afflictions of the gospel according to the power of God; who hath saved us, and called us with a holy calling, not according to our works, but according to his own purpose and grace, which was given us in Christ Jesus before the world began,...."* 2 Timothy 1:7-9.

Paul a disciple of Jesus Christ wrote those words in a letter to his friend and fellow believer Timothy while imprisoned in Rome. He was reminding Timothy that he must persevere and endure for the sake of the spreading of the gospel and for the building up of the body of believers in Christ Jesus. In studying the life of Paul, you learn that he fought and won spiritual battles throughout his Christian walk. Paul traveled his course having his eyes fixed on Jesus. He did not allow himself to fall into tempting situations or look back on his wretched past life. Paul stayed on his course without detouring from any hard places he came to. Paul stayed strong, focused, and accomplished all he was called to do. All the original believers in God's Word are examples of what you must be in Christ from generation to generation.

Disciples demonstrate the love of Christ: John who was at the crucifixion and later became a disciple wrote his first letter to diverse churches in order to confirm that these churches were adhering to the Word of God through the love of God toward man. John writes, *"Beloved, let us love one another; for love is from God; and everyone that loveth is born of God and knoweth God."* 1 John 4:7. In John 13:35, the gospel written by the apostle John, also known as John the Beloved, wrote these words spoken by Jesus, *"By this shall all men know that ye are loved. Charity* [love] *suffered long, and is kind; charity* [love] *envieth not; charity* [love] *vaunted* [to brag] *not itself, is not puffed up, doth not behave itself unseeingly, seeketh not her own, is not easily provoked, thinketh no evil; rejoiceth not in iniquity but rejoiceth in the truth; beareth all things, believeth all things, hopeth all things, endureth all things . Charity* [love] *never faileth: but whether there be prophecies, they shall fail; whether there be tongues, they shall cease; whether there be knowledge, it shall vanish away."* This is God's instruction for his people through Christ Jesus.

Disciples bear the cross of Jesus: Jesus very clearly states in Luke 14:27, *"And whosoever doeth not bear his cross, and come after me, cannot be my disciple."* Living a life in Christ Jesus and for the sake of Christ will cause one to have to bear scrutiny. Christ was degraded. By the world's standards, it is shameful, disgraceful, and humiliating to be a disciple of Jesus Christ let alone a Christian. Many shy away from speaking to others about Christ, the Word of God, and even Salvation, yet you have been called for this purpose. Maybe you have not yet found the path or ways that God would have you use to accomplish his will. Maybe you just need some encouragement or confidence. Whatever your need is trust in God to complete his work through you to fulfill your need. Remember, *"Jesus is the way, the truth, and the life."John 14:6.* Jesus Christ is with you always.

Disciples forsake self to abide in Christ Jesus: *"So likewise, whosoever of you that forsaketh not all that he hath, he cannot be my disciple."* Luke 14:33. Being a disciple of Jesus is like one who leaves all behind to go to war. You leave all your possessions behind to fight for your country believing that what you left behind will be there when you return. You simply trust that all will be well. Jesus wants you to do the same for the sake of the building up of his kingdom and the body of believers. You cannot expect to be able to take your possessions with you. You cannot serve two masters. Christ tells us that through him and in him, you will have all you need in this world including your heart's desire. John 15:7 says, *"If ye abide in me, and my words abide in you, ye shall ask whatever ye will, and it shall be done unto you."* To abide means to bear, endure, and withstand the forces of evil. To stay in solitude with Jesus; maintaining continual fervent prayer and communion daily, regardless of your busy life, outward circumstances, or inner emotions. You must discipline yourself to persevere in Christ, and then you will have answered prayer. To be a disciple of Jesus Christ means to conform to the things of God not of this world. Are you living the life of a disciple of Jesus Christ?

1. Do the choices you make bring you closer to God or draw your attention away from God?

2. Do the people you associate with allow you to speak freely of Jesus Christ in their presence, having fellowship and communion one with another?

3. Are you focused on the things of this world or on the things of God?

4. Are you doing God's work or God's will for your life? The work of God never ends. However, Satan will attempt to keep you busy in the work of God in order to prevent you from doing the will of God for your life. It is important that you have a balance and not forsake God's will for your individual purpose in this world. If it is the call of God on your life to fulfill a particular need, then do it, knowing God has called you to do so. If it is a need, you feel you should take on because no one else will, then examine your motive. You are to fulfill God's will and purpose for your life and pray for God to send someone to provide for the need that is not yours to fill. Help temporarily if God leads you to. You will know God is leading you because his leading follows his peace, which enters and dwells inside you. Temporarily assist with a need until you know your true calling and the right time to fulfill it.

5. How much time do you spend daily in God's Word and in prayer?

There is a separation between the things of this world and the things of God. God will not force you to draw closer to him he will just patiently wait for you, hoping you will come and be his disciple. His eyes continually roam the earth hoping and waiting because he knows you can do more. God has programmed you to succeed. You are more than able to fulfill your destiny in him. Just believe all things are possible through Jesus Christ.

*Chapter 4*

# The Many Faces of Hope
**A True Story**

❧❦❧

Although our family appeared normal to those around us, the struggles between my parents grew increasingly worse. My father was coming home later and later. There were arguments about his drinking habits, money for bills, and a woman named Joan. These were matters too difficult for a young child to understand. Having one older brother and three younger sisters the lives of five young children were about to change forever. Suddenly our father was gone with the exception of an occasional visit to our house. There were no more Sunday family trips to the local bakery for rolls and donuts while mom stayed home to make the bacon and eggs. Welfare became our lifeline. Families within the neighborhood provided hand-me-down clothes for us to wear. I was eleven, my brother twelve, and my sisters were nine, eight, and a newborn. Succumbed with anger, disappointment, and the pressure of working nights, my mother eventually drove herself into severe depression and a frenzy of madness she released unto her children. Faced with failure, rejection, a lack of security, and the stress of raising five young children alone my mother increased her wine consumption. The alcohol numbed her pain. Nevertheless, it would not be long before she was angry again. Her methods for punishment became increasingly abusive toward us. I knew there was love in her. She just changed along with the rest of us. Sometimes I would see love in her as she covered her face and sobbed aloud after talking to my father on the phone. Occasionally the expression of love was in a smile of approval after speaking to a neighbor out in the yard. Nevertheless, the weight of responsibility fell on me the oldest daughter of five children. By and by, my mother's sorrows multiplied. The burden had become too heavy for her to bear. She tried to hide her pain at the bar she worked in or behind a bottle of wine at home. Eventually, my mother purchased her own bar and had it set up in the family room. She began having holiday parties and other celebrations throughout the year. Although my mother appeared happier to the outside world her secret life of abuse toward her children had increased especially toward me her oldest daughter. Now an adult I look back remembering the rolling pin she bent while hitting one sister on the head and a broken pipe she hit another sister with in the back of her leg. Then there were the countless hairbrushes, shoes, and not to mention the two by four taken from the garage she used on me in front of my girlfriend who lived right next door. We had just walked in the front door from school. It was sixth grade my mother who was waiting just inside the door began yelling and swinging at me with what appeared to be about three feet of wood from the garage. Frequently my mother would use whatever she could get her hands on for what she justified as punishment. My girlfriend wasn't allowed to come over to my house anymore after that day.

Throughout my childhood, I imagined black prison bars on the window above my bed. Black prison bars reflecting entrapment to my secret life of abuse, fear, and the absence of love. Many times, I climbed onto my bed and buried my head deep into my pillow to muffle the sound of my sobs as I wondered why. Why did she hurt me again? Why is she always yelling? What did I do wrong? Suddenly I heard sounds coming from outside my window. Lifting my head from my pillow, I pulled myself up toward the window. Grimly I gazed through the imaginary black prison bars as little tear-stained eyes peered out toward the empty lot across the street wondering what was on the other side of the treetops. Where there houses with kids playing happily and a dog running in the yard? Would a kind woman's smiling face lean forward with arms stretched out offering me a great big hug? Is it safe out there? Are the people nice? What would I find? What would I see? I imagined a life free of pain and full of love. Hearing about God's love during an occasional Sunday Mass gave me hope and strength to believe that God was watching over me. At night, I would seek God's smiling face in the moon and talk to him. It made me feel loved and accepted by God. As I grew I blindly trusted in the kind faces of others passing through my life; guests invited to our house, people at the grocery store, and our neighbors, to mention a few. I believed in the expressions of joy seen in the faces of the kids at the corner bus stop, on the school playground, and in the faces of my schoolteachers. With the exception of my fifth grade teacher, none of the faces I saw had any of the cold stern facial expressions my mother wore behind closed doors. The faces of those looking at me did not yell at me. I liked school and loved God. God allowed me to see joy through the faces of others, which gave me hope for my life. I counted the long years in silent persistence of my hopes and dreams. Then one day I knew it was time to put hope into action and just believe. I was in eleventh grade when it happened. My mother was standing by the stove and I was standing by the kitchen table when she started yelling at me again. Taken by surprise I found myself contemplating the thought of making a serious and major decision in my life. Do I turn to my right and run or take another beating with who knows what she might find in the kitchen cabinet this time. You see, according to my mother the meal I cooked consisting of fish sticks, french-fries, and corn was not suitable for my brother and sisters to eat for dinner. Trembling from head to toe, my stomach in knots, and contemplation whether to stay and take another beating or run out the kitchen door I chose to run. I pivoted right flew to the door pushed it open and ran as fast as I could through the dark of night across the front yard toward my boyfriend's car. He was picking me up, as previously planned and approved by my mother, to go to a movie. My mother knew he was waiting outside for me. I ran for my life hysterically shouting, "GO! GO! GO!" as I dove through the open window of his car. Confused and frightened Mark quickly glanced toward me and floored the gas pedal as he turned to watch the road. I made my way completely into the car as he took off down the road and around the corner. Mark already knew of my family life and wanted to help. Little did he know of how or when his help would come. It was a long and scary night. I hid not knowing what to do next. Did I plan to heave home this way? No but I could tell in my mother's eyes that she had plans for a severe beating that night. I just decided not to get hurt any more. The school tried to help in years past. One time the school spoke to a social worker. The social worker came to our house asked us questions and then asked our neighbors a few questions. We all sat at the kitchen table together with my mother present as the social worker proceeded to ask us many questions. No one said a word. Even when the social worker asked my mother to leave the table no one said a word. I am sure you can guess why. No one was willing to say anything not even the neighbors who knew from the resonating shouts of my mother's anger throughout the house as she hit or beat upon us. The neighbors knew because the loud cries heard outside the house drew the attention of the children playing nearby. One day my mother beat my sister with a rolling pin. I could not bear to watch so I went outside by the garage doors and cried. Under my cries, I could hear the whisper of children laughing in the background. I turned to see some of our neighbor's children, our friends, in our back yard trying to watch through the sliding glass doors as they laughed. With tears streaming down my face I shouted, "Get away from there, and get out of there!" As I watched them run off laughing, I could not believe their reaction to what was happening in my home. Then I noticed dead silence filled the air. I slowly and silently went back into the house hoping my mother would not notice that I went outside without her permission. I looked for my sister Sandi to find her desperately attempting to carry a full load of clean folded laundry up the stairs to our bedrooms. My mother came out of the family room holding out toward me the bent rolling pin she just finished using on Sandi as she said, "Don't you help her or you will be next. She is being punished." I looked back toward Sandi with much sorrow wishing I could take her pain away. She was always the strong one in our house. She just kept her head up as best as she could trying not to let any more tears flow from her eyes as she turned to persistently make her way up two levels of stairs with a full load of clean folded laundry. I do not know why none of our neighbors would help us. No one was willing to get involved.

A few years later while standing in the kitchen with the threat of another beating I chose to take matters into my own hands and leave home. About two weeks after leaving home my mother wanted to see me and I needed some things from my room. God used my older brother and a few of his friends to help me. He knew of our mother's abusive behaviors even though he was rarely subject to them. Not knowing if this was a trap set by my mother, my brother helped me by gathering together several of his friends. Some were those laughing kids from our neighborhood who were older now. They formed a military defense line across our front lawn. My brother told me to stand several feet behind the line and so I did. My mother came to the front door assuring my safety to everyone and to my sisters who were inside. As I walked into the house, my mother immediately locked all the doors of the house. My trembling body wanted to run. However, I also wanted to trust her. Therefore, I just stood perfectly still hoping I was safe. From where I was standing, I could see through the windows of the house. I saw my brother and his friends running toward every entrance of the house. They were ready to break in at a moment's notice. I feared my life but also felt protected by my brother and his friends. My mother invited me away from the front door and into the kitchen where we stood and talked a little when suddenly the phone rang. It was my grandmother. Not understanding

Spanish I just stood in the middle of the kitchen floor waiting for her to finish on the phone. While still talking my mother suddenly screamed. My brother thinking that I screamed broke through the outside screen of the sliding doors in the living room. Trying to break open the inside glass door my sisters told him that I was safe and to wait outside. Then I heard shouts from the neighborhood kids outside wanting to know what was happening. Though I trembled with fear, I knew I was not getting a beating this time. In the end, I was able to get some things from my room. I shared a room with my younger sister Sandi who came upstairs with me to our room. She said that because I left home she now understood what I went through as the oldest daughter who bore the weight of responsibility for everyone and its consequences. With deep remorse, I told her that I was very sorry to put her in this situation and to be careful. Sadly, I left the room carrying a bag or two down the stairs and out the front door without another word spoken to anyone. My mother must have brought my sisters into the family room with her as I left. Part of that moment is a bluer.

Now a teenage runaway scared and unsure of anything I kept my mind focused on what I saw in the faces of others, peace, love, joy, acceptance, and the hope for a healthier and happier way of life. God used my imagination to keep hope alive in me during those difficult years. Though I did not know God very well, he knew me and waited for me to come to know him. There were those who tried to tell me about God and Jesus but I did not understand how God could help me. Growing up I simply believed that he loved me. Little did I know that upon receiving Jesus into my heart my life would change forever. Looking back on my childhood I realized that the abuse I suffered was not a part of God's plan. I learned that when I cried God cried too. Being able to understand my childhood and growing years meant seeing my life through the eyes of Jesus Christ. It meant letting go of trying to find all the answers and pressing forward. It meant leaving my past at the cross and moving on with the rest of my life. The memories are there and always will be. I may even tremble from time to time as I hear a child going through a similar situation. A part of me longs to be that kind faced woman leaning forward with her arms stretched out offering all children a great big hug. However, I want you to know the journey through life as a runaway was just as difficult as my childhood years. I do not recommend running away to anyone.

If you find yourself in a challenging situation that you have no control over, then seek help and strive for change. Change your surroundings. Act in faith, have hope, and trust in God. Speak out the things in life you hope for get on your knees pray earnestly and believe, believe, believe. Have hope in your dreams and act upon them by faith. Faith births assurance to believe in truth, to hope in dreams, to help establish trustworthiness in others, and the will to succeed in whatever you do. True faith and hope in God means that a person has total assurance in giving God control of his or her life. The assurance of things to come does not rest on logical proof or material evidence; but strictly by what is unseen and by total faith and hope in God and in His Word. *"Now faith is the evidence of things hoped for and the conviction of things not seen."* Hebrews 11:1.

The instant I chose to leave home I did not know what my life would bring, how I would live, or where my next meal would come from. I just made a decision based on the circumstances of that moment. I went forth into the world blindly and learned to trust in God. I could not hide at my boyfriend's house for long. His father did not want to get involved especially with a minor. In addition, my mother was calling Mark's family every hour through the night harassing the family until seven am the next morning. She did this for days threatening to get the police involved. Mark and I eventually broke up. He enlisted in the army. All I could do was pray. Though I spent some nights in the streets and eating second hand meals, I knew God had just the right place for me; it was just a matter of his perfect timing. Moreover, when that time came God did bless me and blessed me abundantly. A family took me in as their own, helped to get me into college, taught me how to drive, and set my feet on a healthier and happier path in life. God provided for all my needs.

## Chapter 5

# From Faith to Freedom

 ✦

In the Old Testament, we read that Abel gave better offer-ings to God than Cain. How God took Enoch to heaven where Enoch never saw death, Genesis 5. Noah built an ark. Abraham left his country and relatives to go to an unknown promised land. Sara conceived in her old age. Moses parted the red sea. Joshua obeyed God by faith. The walls of Jericho came down and many kingdoms were conquered. In the New Testament Peter walked on water. The disciples cast out devils, healed the sick, and fed great multitudes. Mary Magdalene, a prostitute, accepted Jesus Christ as her Lord and Savior. Though neither of us was present for any of these miraculous events in history by faith we believe they took place. By faith, we accept Jesus Christ as our Lord and Savior yet we were not there to see him nailed to the cross and put to death. By faith, we expect to receive from God. We cannot see faith. We do not know how God will deliver his promise to us. However, we know by faith that what we ask for in him will happen. Faith is the act of choosing to place all our hope and trust in God the Father, God the Son, and God the Holy Spirit to fulfill all we ask for in him. Faith and hope strengthen and fill the believer's soul with the assurance of a more abundant life through Jesus Christ our Lord and Savior. By faith, we believe God's Word and all that he created.

Paul openly proclaimed to all people that they must hear the Gospel of Jesus Christ in order to believe in it. He preached that God is the same Lord to all people and Lord over all, that Jesus is gracious and merciful. God delivered Paul from being a hater and murderer of Christians to a disciple of Jesus Christ. However, Paul first needed to hear the God's Word. Paul's name was Saul before his encounter with Jesus. Jesus visited Saul when Saul was on the road to Damascus with a written order to kill many Christians. Jesus said, *"Saul, Saul, why persecutest thou me? I am Jesus whom thou persecutest, arise and go into the city, and it shall be told thee what thou must do,"* Acts 9:4-6. Saul learned that Christ is the promised Messiah and that God's Word is truth. Saul accepted this revelation and believed in it by faith. Then God redeemed (rescued) Saul and changed his name from Saul to Paul. His life transformed from a murderer and persecutor of Christians to an evangelist and minister of God's Word. God gives to all who call on him through Jesus Christ our Lord and Savior. *"Faith cometh by hearing and hearing by the word of God."* Romans 10:17.

In order to receive from God you must call on him through Jesus Christ your Lord and Savior. *"For there is one God, and one mediator between God and men, the man Christ Jesus; who gave himself a ransom for all, to be testified in due time."* 1Timothy 2:5-6. Your life in Christ is to be lived in constant prayer and communication with God through Jesus Christ your Lord and Savior. The message Paul brought to the Gentiles, *"that if thou shalt confess with thy mouth the Lord Jesus, and shalt believe in thine heart that God raised him from the dead, thou shalt be saved. For with the heart man believeth, unto righteousness; and with the mouth confession is made unto salvation."* Romans 10:9-10. *"Whosoever shall call upon the name of the Lord shall be saved."* Romans 10:13. Paul tried to explain this point to the Jews by asking three questions:

1. How can anyone call upon him whom he or she does not believe in?
2. How can anyone believe in him whom he or she has not heard about?
3. How can anyone hear about Jesus Christ without the presence of a teacher?

Paul's intention was to bring the Gentiles within reach of the promise of God. The Gentiles must first believe that

Jesus Christ is Lord of all before being able to call upon him for Salvation. In order for the Gentiles to believe, they had to hear God's Word. In order to hear God's Word, God had to send a teacher, preacher, or messenger of the Good News. Paul continued to preach to the Gentiles and many were saved. Today more Gentiles have accepted Jesus Christ as their Lord and Savior than Jews. *"For so hath the Lord commanded us, saying, I have set thee to be a light of the Gentiles, that thou shouldest be for salvation unto the ends of the earth,"* Acts 13:47. Romans 10:9-10, 13 above does not mean that everyone who quotes this scripture is saved. Remember, there are three parts to verses 9, 10, and 13. Romans 10:14-15 mentions the three parts.

1. How does one call upon him whom they do not believe in? The lost must first believe that Christ died for their sins, was buried, and resurrected on the third day for the redemption of sin. Then the lost are found through Christ Jesus. Those who do not believe in the death, burial, and resurrection of Christ Jesus according to God's Word, do not accept him as their Lord and Savior.

2. How shall anyone believe in him whom he or she has not heard of? The answer is that no one believes in what he or she does not know. The Bible gives us examples of those who heard and believed. Acts chapter eight tells us the story of an Ethiopian Eunuch,

a court official who was in charge of the queens treasures. He went to Jerusalem to worship God. On his return trip Philip, a disciple of Jesus Christ, was called of God to visit the Eunuch. The Eunuch asked Philip to explain the passage of scripture he was reading in Isaiah where a man was led as a sheep to slaughter. Therefore, here is an example of a man who went to Jerusalem to worship but did not know Jesus. Philip spoke to the Eunuch about Christ's life, death, burial, and resurrection. The Eunuch believed upon hearing. The Eunuch then asked to be water baptized. Philip baptized the Eunuch in the name of Jesus Christ. From there the Eunuch continued his journey rejoicing in his newly found life and salvation through Jesus Christ. Acts chapter nine tells us the story of Paul previously called Saul who also had to hear in order to believe. Saul learned that the authenticity and ministry of Jesus Christ was very real. This event in history goes on to tell us that Saul, upon hearing the Word of God, accepted Jesus Christ as his Lord and Savior, was healed of temporary blindness, stayed with the disciples and began preaching in the Synagogues. God knew that in Saul's heart he wanted to know and believe the truth. Saul, whose name Jesus changed to Paul, had a tremendous ministry preaching to the Gentiles.

In Acts chapter ten we read a story of how God sent Peter a Jew and disciple of Jesus Christ to a Gentiles home whose name was Cornelius. Cornelius was a devout man who feared God, gave generously to the poor, and both Cornelius and his household prayed continually. Peter spoke the Good News of Jesus Christ to all who were present in Cornelius' house. As he was speaking, the Holy Spirit fell upon all those who were listening to the messages, both the Jews who came with Peter and the Gentiles. All the people began speaking in tongues and exalting God. They all received the baptism of the Holy Spirit and were water baptized in the name of Jesus Christ of Nazareth.

3. How shall they hear without a preacher? There must be some way of hearing the Word of God in order to have the opportunity to believe and receive Salvation through the acceptance of Jesus Christ. The Eunuch received salvation through Philip who interpreted the scriptures that gave the Eunuch understanding. Cornelius and his entire household received salvation through Peter who bore witness to them. Paul preached to the Gentiles even at the opposition of the Jews for the sake of those who might accept Christ as he did. All receive salvation that hear, confess, believe, and receive the Word of God through faith in Jesus Christ of Nazareth, the greatest witness and

preacher that ever lived. Remember, Romans 10:17, *"Faith cometh by hearing and hearing by the Word of God."* Faith brings salvation through Jesus Christ. *"If thou shalt confess with thy mouth the Lord Jesus, and shalt believe in thine heart that God hath raised him from the dead, thou shalt be saved,"* Romans 10:9.

Your soul is fed by reading and meditating on God's Word. Daily you receive and digest assurance, trust, expectation, confidence, loyalty, truth, conviction, unwavering dedication, and devotion to God through Jesus Christ and by faithfully reading God's Word. Input into your mind, body, and soul comes from what you see, hear, and believe. The more time spent in God's Word and prayer the greater the manifestation of his will and the stronger you become in him. The application of faith manifests itself through determination. Standing your ground on what you know and believe to be true before God. You must openly confess with your mouth the truth of the Gospel that becomes deeply rooted in your heart if you truly believe. As believers, you must openly bear witness that Jesus Christ is your Lord and Savior that you depend on him for all things and that without him you are nothing and have nothing.

God requires that you confess Jesus Christ as your Lord and Savior before all men. God also requires that you believe in your heart that He raised Jesus Christ from the dead. Confessing Jesus with your mouth alone is not enough. Without the energy or driving force within you to believe in your heart that God raised Jesus Christ from the dead, your faith is dead and your belief in the resurrection of Jesus Christ is a mockery. A Christian's belief relies on the resurrection of Jesus Christ or there would be no salvation for all humanity. It is very important to God that both confession and belief take place. Therefore, there must first be faith in your heart to believe in order for there to be confession from your mouth acceptable and pleasing to God. What is in your heart and confessed with your mouth relies on the consent of your own will to accept or not to accept the things of God through Jesus Christ your Lord and Savior. God makes it very clear that by confessing with your mouth you sacrifice your self-will and your body unto him. Moreover, by believing in your heart you give your soul unto him through faith in Jesus Christ. God also wants to see that by believing in Jesus Christ from your heart you will not be ashamed to confess him with your mouth. God wants to see that you are not embarrassed or unwilling to confess your hope and belief in Jesus Christ. If you abide by these things in faith through Jesus Christ then you have received Salvation. *"Have faith in God."* Mark 11:22. *"Thy faith hath saved thee; go in peace."* Luke 7:50.

You cannot live in Christ or be used of God without faith. God does not call upon you to look at who you are. He does not see you the same way you see yourself. God sees beyond the natural man into the supernatural man in you. God sees your potential in him. If he can change Paul from a murderer to a preacher and evangelist, consider what he can do for you. You need to see yourself through the eyes of God not man. If he can take Matthew, a dishonest tax collector and politician who partook in riotous living and make him one of Jesus disciples, consider what he can do for you. Mary Magdalene was demon possessed and a prostitute who transformed her life and became the first woman disciple proclaiming Jesus' resurrection. Peter denied Jesus three times repented and God used his shadow to heal the sick. Doubting Thomas was insecure. Samson had long hair. Noah got drunk. Moses committed murder and disobeyed God. Sarah was barren for almost one hundred years before giving birth to Isaac. Ruth was a destitute widow until God blessed her according to her faith. Miriam became a leper after criticizing her brother Moses, an anointed man of God. Then God forgave Miriam, cured her, and she became a prophetess. Deborah, Huldah, Isaiah's wife, Anna, and Philip's daughters were prophetesses.

God also used many children. In his youth, God called Joseph to become a very powerful man and overseer in Egypt. As a child, Samuel heard God's choice and had prophetic visions. God anointed David, son of Jesse who later became a great king. Josiah became king of Judah at eight years old. The orphan girl, Hadassah, adopted by her uncle Mordecai, later became Queen Ester. Daniel interpreted dreams and had great wisdom. Before his birth, God called John the Baptist to prepare the way for the coming of the Messiah. The point is this, if God can take unworthy sinners of all ages, from all generations, and all walks of life; forgive them of their sins, renew their minds, their souls, and their spirit, to use them to help further his kingdom, then he can most certainly use you. God tells us in his word that all has sinned and fall short of his glory. God is slow to anger, merciful, and forgiving. Your Lord God needs you. All he requires is a little faith in him. It does not matter where you have been or what you have done. What matters is "here and now." This very moment you need to ask yourself where you want to be in your life with God. What do you want to accomplish? It is time to stop sitting on the sidelines of life out of fear, depression, rejection, insecurity, pride, the unknown, or any other distraction preventing you from moving ahead with Jesus. Stop allowing the enemy to run amuck in your mind. Begin exercising a little child-like faith. Then watch it grow to new heights in your life through Jesus Christ. *"Because of your unbelief: for verily I say unto you, If ye have faith as a grain of mustard seed, ye shall say unto this mountain, remove hence to yonder place; and it shall remove; and nothing shall be impossible unto you."* Matthew 17:20.

**Believe in the Impossible**

Believe it can happen without an occupation.

Believe it can happen without an education.

Believe it can happen without a bank loan.

Believe it can happen no matter what critics may say.

Believe in the Lord God who does the impossible.

*By Susan DeRienzo*

## Chapter 6

# In Search Of Love

❧❀❧

*"By night on my bed I sought him whom my soul loveth: I sought him, but I found him not. I will rise now, and go about the city in the streets, and in the broad ways I will seek him whom my soul loveth: I sought him, but I found him not."* Song of Solomon 3:12.

Many seek love in the security and acceptance of others as if another person can fulfill that deep longing for true love. This compelling need creates a deep desire to do whatever it takes to receive love. So the prowl begins in search of what you believe will satisfy that innate yearning for love. The passage of scripture above portrays a woman searching for her lover. Have you ever wanted something so bad that you would do anything to get it? You sweat and sacrifice to prove your self-worth, offer a promise of fulfillment and satisfaction to stay together; you are willing to do whatever it takes to receive love. Likewise, you may think that you have found love in that special someone by the twinkle in his eye, that certain easy lightheaded feeling when you are together, the lack of concentration in daily routines, or in that special attention you've always desired that makes you feel valued, appreciated, and accepted. You say that this is the one, tie the knot, and your marriage begins. Life is bliss. You share intimate affections and rely on each other for personal satisfaction. The years pass. Change is guaranteed to take place. You could almost read each other's thoughts and become more comfortable in your daily routine. The twinkle in his eye is gone along with the blissful feelings of weightlessness. More years pass. Kind words with understanding change to ridicule and sarcasm. The love and acceptance of each other turn to a lack of self-worth and heartache. Fulfillment replaced with isolation and emptiness. Why, because only God's unconditional love truly fulfills the heart of a man or a woman. The key word is unconditional.

Unconditional love means to commit oneself without guarantee. It is an act of faith. Love is trustworthy and gives without expecting in return. Love requires a sacrifice of your will. You must want to entrust and communicate your dedication and devotion toward helping to make a difference. *"Though I speak with the tongues of men and of angels, and have not charity* [love], *I am become as sounding brass, or a tinkling cymbal. And though I have the gift of prophecy, and understand all mysteries and all knowledge, and though*

*I have all faith, so that I could remove mountains, and have not charity* [charity], *I am nothing. And though I bestow all my goods to feed the poor, and though I give my body to be burned, and have not charity* [love], *it profiteth me nothing. Charity* [love] *suffereth long, and is kind; and is not puffed up* [jealous], *does not behave itself unseemingly; seeketh not her own, is not easily provoked, thinketh no evil; but rejoiceth in the truth; beareth all things, believeth all things, hopeth all things, endureth all things. Charity* [love] *never fails."* 1 Corinthians 13:1-8.

Consider this fact about love. The ability to love others and still have love in you means that love was designed and created to be shared not just given. Love sustains itself within you while simultaneously giving love to another. Therefore, love when given to another still remains in you. This is one of God's great miracles. Love given is actually love shared. There is no need to search for love outside on one's self or outside of God. God placed love inside of you when he created you. Let's take a second look at Song of Solomon Chapter 3:1-2. *"By night on my bed I sought him whom my soul loveth. I sought him, but I found him not. I will rise now, and go about the city in the streets, and in the broad ways, I will seek him whom my soul loveth. I sought him, but I found him not."* In the natural, this understanding of God's Word appears very clear. The most common interpretation is that of human nature, a woman in search of her missing lover. When she sees that he is not at home, she gets up in the night and goes out in search of him because of her great love for him. Looking deeper and expanding our thoughts allows for the spiritual understanding of this passage of scripture. *"On my bed night after night I sought him whom my **soul** loves. I sought him but did not find him…"* What do you do at night? You pray in your bed or kneel beside it and search your soul for answers. You seek God to find *"Him whom your **soul** loves."* You search for Jesus in your life and the love he placed in your heart. You deeply examine the thoughts of your mind, the actions you have taken towards others, and your motives for these actions. You search your inner being asking questions. Does your daily living line up with Godly living? Do you feel God's presents near you or is it as if he does not hear you? Does this time of prayer feel as if God is not listening or as if his presence is gone from your life? Then you ask yourself, "What can I do to make things right with God?" It is mostly in times of despair you search your mind for the heart of God even more. As expressed in Song of Solomon, you cannot live without love especially God's love. You are incomplete without God's unconditional love. The understanding of this scripture is that true believers will pray and seek God's love and compassion. If you cannot find God's love then you search your heart and the scriptures continually until you find it, just as one without love may search elsewhere for love. A truly devoted child of God will study God's Word for answers and ponder these thoughts. "Where did I go wrong? What did I do to go astray? How can I feel God's love again?" You come to realize that the answer was inside you all along. Your need for love cannot be satisfied by another. Remember, God put his great love in you when he created you. All you need to do is a little **soul** searching to find it. *"Seek and ye shall find."* Moreover, the gates of heaven will pour out God's unconditional love from inside of you in abundance. *"Ask and it shall be given you; seek and ye shall find; knock and it shall be opened unto you."* Matthew 7:7.

Love sustains itself and generates its own energy in a way similar to the sun. Have you ever wondered how the sun feeds and strengthens itself to light up the sky and warn our atmosphere? God originally made the sun from a spinning cloud of gaseous elements called a nebula. Its enormous size is 875,000 miles in diameter weighing 333,000 times more than Earth. This great star has an energy force field so powerful that it only takes eight minutes for its light to reach Earth, which is 93 million miles away. The point is this, as big and powerful as the sun is, its core must contain certain elements for the sun to perform with such magnitude. There elements must work together vigorously with enormous strength and power to accomplish what it was designed by God to do. Another example of energy generated from within is the making of a cake. The ingredients by themselves accomplish nothing. Mix the ingredients together and a chemical change occurs creating a new substance called batter. You pour the batter into a baking pan and place the pan into a pre-heated oven to await another chemical change, a delicious solid mass. Just as the core elements of our great sun must work together to produce sunshine and warmth for our planet, the ingredients for a cake must work together to change liquid to a solid emitting a wonderful and appetizing aroma that draws everyone's attention. Add the finishing touches and the outcome is a beautiful and delicious work of art.

What you allow to enter into your core being are the ingredients used to create love. Then you make an independent decision on how to use and share love with others. Just as the sun peers through the clouds creating a dry, warm, beautiful sunny day, you are to press through the clouds of human despair to lighten the burdens in your way. You see, love knows no difference between right and wrong or good and evil. You are in control of what you allow to penetrate through to your inner being. The core of your inner being works the same way as the sun's core or the core ingredients used to make a cake. Your core being is your **soul**. Your soul requires certain elements working together to produce unconditional love in you. When these elements are working together, warmth from your heart emits the aroma of love towards others unconditionally.

Let's look at some ingredients needed to have unconditional love. Your inner being thrives on healthy nourishment. Now you can speak in terms of healthy foods to eat but I am speaking of healthy input and output to your soul. When searching for love it is vitally important that you are aware of your surroundings, the people you associate with and your relationship with God. God has equipped you with the ability to reach beyond the existence of your present environment, to soar higher in your position at work, to live in your dream home, to break away from the status-quo; seeing yourself where you want to be living in abundance. You may feel overwhelmed by life but God can change your present circumstances by the work you allow him to do in you. Placing yourself in a healthy environment gives you your own space and quality time with God. For some, your environment (privacy) may be limited to the solitude of a bedroom. For others it may be in a bathroom behind locked doors or in a car where no one else can hear you talk to God. Maybe physically relocating would offer a new beginning. Break away from the status-quo. Reach beyond your comfort zone. Associate with people who encourage you, people who are successful wise and full of faith in God. Watch how change and prosperity will rub off from those around you onto you. Remember, we become a product of our environment. If you do not like whom you are, or the negative influences of those around you then make some changes. Take advantage of small opportunities that come your way. Stay focused on your dreams. Do not let other people's failures put doubt into your mind. Steer away from negative minded people. As you begin to make these changes, you are feeding your soul healthy nourishment needed to develop and emanate unconditional love. Rise above your present circumstances by embracing your vision for life. Focus on making your dreams a reality. This is all a part of sifting out the bad from the good in your life to allow for healthier input into your soul. You need to replace all unhealthiness with positive-mindedness, encouragement, motivation for success, and a healthy self-image, which says, **"I deserve the best. I am a child of the most high God. All that is his is mine through inheritance."** *"In whom also we have obtained an inheritance, being predestinated according to the purpose of him who worketh all things after the counsel of his own will."* Ephesians 1:11. *"Blessed are the meek, for they shall inherit the earth."* Matthew 5:5. *"But the meek shall inherit the earth; and shall delight themselves in the abundance of peace."* Psalms 37:11.

God wants nothing less than his best for you. However, his best first begins with you by keeping a Godly attitude and expecting God's favor in your life. He will help you turn obstacles into opportunities with purpose and meaning. God already sees you as an over-comer. You must see yourself the same way. Begin to fill your inner being, your soul, with healthy ingredients in order for a change to take place. Sift out what does not belong. Steer away from all things that cause weakness in your character. Do not take in ridicule or negative-mindedness from others. Everyone has weaknesses. Let us not feed them. Put your life in God's hands. Stop trying to figure everything out. God already drew the blueprints for your life. Take one day at a time. Do not expect your day to go your way. Learn to expect the unexpected with gratitude for what GOD is doing to help you become the best YOU, you are called by God to be. Try not to think so much. Do not even consider putting yourself in a tempting situation. Let go of the control you have over your life. Let God love you one day at a time, step-by-step, moment-by-moment. Change your thinking to help develop a healthier self-image, strength of character, and confidence in that whatever you touch will prosper. Most of all, allow God's unconditional love to reign in your life. God does the impossible and wants to turn your obstacles into opportunities, trials into triumphs, stumbling blocks into stepping-stones, and stress into strength in Christ Jesus.

Be positive minded. Learn to care for others even when you don't feel like it. Do sacrificial acts of selflessness. Learn to be patient, accepting that you are on God's time clock not your own. Be honest before God in your dealings with others, especially with those who are not very honest with you. Instill these values into your soul as ingredients working together to create God's unconditional love. It is the input needed in your body, mind, and soul; like the elements of the sun, which attributes to a thermonuclear reaction. Learn to generate from within what you know is right before God. Your prayer time with God, reading scriptures, and being associated with the right people are where you will find the ingredients for true unconditional love.

*Chapter 7*

# Peace I Leave With You

※⊙※

There is no one on earth who knows all the deep secrets of your heart. No other can feel the way you do or see life through your eyes. Your character and personality are unique and of great value to God. You are like no other person in the world. God created only one of you. He created your uniqueness because he needs you just the way he made you. The decisions you make and the direction you take in life is strictly yours to choose. Nevertheless, God needs you to live up to his standards not societies. Start by learning to accept and appreciate your uniqueness. Search your heart striving to be the wonderful person you know you are on the inside. Let that person out even if it means standing alone in what you believe.

At eight years old, an ice-cream truck hit my husband resulting in a broken leg. He had to wear a cast for ten months. Throughout that year, his body continued to grow, all except his leg in the cast. He struggled through childhood with one leg four inches shorter than the other and with being overweight. In spite of the obstacles and ridicules, he made friends and still managed to play sports in school. Choosing to go to work to help his mother, my husband never completed ninth grade. Nevertheless, a lack of education did not stop him from building his own very successful auto dealership and becoming an ordained minister. Pastor Rocky DeRienzo later founded Full Gospel Bible Church, a non-denominational church in North Belmore, New York. My husband strived beyond his limitations even when it meant standing alone for what he believed in about himself. Jesus sets no boundaries to maximize your potential. He longs for you to soar like an eagle above the clouds to where there is peace and serenity. Jesus calls you to let go of the past and rise above your circumstances, above the clouds of despair, confusion, and difficulty. To distance yourself from all that opposes peace. Jesus said, *"Peace I leave with you, my peace I give unto you."* John 14:27.

*A True Story*

"Where are you going? You get over here right now!" demanded her mother. Fear stricken and trembling, Victoria's little feet slowly crept toward mother in sobering obedience to her call when suddenly startled by a shout, "NOW!" Frozen stiff, eyes tightly shut; hands clasped together in front of her, Victoria wondered what her next punishment would be and why. Suddenly mother's arms sprang forward grabbing Victoria's arms in a tight squeeze. Then she jerked Victoria forward causing Victoria to lose her balance and fall. Her unsympathetic mother dragged Victoria down the hall yelling, "Where is my coffee? It's Saturday my coffee should have been made by now." Mother's eyes peered down at Victoria sitting on the floor. A fountain of tears streamed down Victoria's cheeks. With trembling lips and silent sobs, Victoria struggled for the breath to say, "I'm sorry mommy." Like a fire-breathing dragon, her mother shook a finger toward Victoria shouting, "You had better get up and make that coffee or else you know what's good for you." Her mother then whisked a cold crisp about face as she headed back to her bedroom to snuggle peacefully under her flowery linen bed covers with her usual contented smile and a sigh of relief in anticipation of a warm soothing cup of coffee after working all night long. In the kitchen, Victoria slowly scrambled to her feet and dried her tears and nose with her pajama sleeve. She then went to the refrigerator for the can of coffee grinds and placed them on the counter. She pulled a chair from the kitchen table to the counter. One knee up then the other, Victoria then reached to the back of the counter with both hands for the coffee pot. She opened it took out the inside parts laid them on the counter and placed the pot in the sink. Reaching way over Victoria turned on the cold water. Through the glistening sparkles of cool water slowly streaming down into the coffee pot, Victoria escaped into the world of her imagination where fun, enchantment, and visions of tranquil wonders pleased the adventurous mind of all little girls. Those brief moments were a place of refuge for Victoria before reaching over the sink to turn the water off. She picked up the coffee pot now filled to the first line with water, placed it on the counter opened the can of coffee placed two scoops of coffee into the filter and put the parts back together again before placing them into the coffee pot. Victoria put the cover on the coffee pot plugged it in and waited as she usually did. Only this time Victoria deliberately reached over to turn on the water again. Her timid sweet face emanated a glow of delight as she stretched her arms towards the cool sparkling water wiggling her fingers through the glistening streams. Once again, Victoria disappeared onto the wings of her imagination; taking her to places full of wonders and secret fantasies. A place filled with rainbow colors, sunshine, peace, and love. Victoria even gave herself this beautiful name pretending to be the happy little girl she believes exists inside of her. Victoria is a name known only to her imagination where it was safe, a name that she allowed to become someone other than a frightened abused child. A princess name representing beauty, radiance, and peace in a child's imaginary world.

At an early age, Victoria learned the art of finding strength from within and from those around her. Through silent persistence, Victoria believed in the examples of her peers at school. She deliberately set out to overcome her circumstances by observing classmates laughing and having confidence in what they did. There seemed to be something right and fun about this, she thought to herself. The kids also made plans to get together after school or on weekends, plans to go to the mall or to parties together. However, Victoria always had to be home from school on time and with not a moment to spare. Repeatedly her mother's threatening eyes peered down with a pointed finger as she distinctly demanded, "If you know what's good for you, you'd better be home on time! I'm watching the clock young lady!"

You see, living in fear and under my mother's constant demands, my special name, Victoria, made me feel like a princess. It helped me to believe in something beyond my immediate circumstances and at times kept me strong. I even imagined myself as the beautiful princess in the children's fairytales who lived happily ever after. As I grew older and more independent, I changed the "ia" in Victoria to "y" from Victoria to Victory. God later showed me how instrumental the name Victoria became in my life. It was a constant reminder of hope in the mind and heart of a small child. It is amazing how God works to protect us and keep us in his tender care. He knew I could not live on my own so he equipped me with the ability to live using strength from within. Jesus was watching over me the whole time. In Jesus, there is victory. So remember that when circumstances around you seem hopeless, turn toward the inside of you to find refuge because *"greater is he that is in you than he that is in the world."* 1John 4:4. God knows you much better than you know yourself. He loves you and continually watches over you. Just believe for greater things than your present circumstances. Call out to him and listen for his response. God will bring you peace in his perfect time. For me, peace began when I removed myself from the source of turmoil, conflict, and abuse. Then my mind began to clear. My heart became more receptive. My will to seek God for help drew me closer to him. It is amazing the peace God gives at just the right time in his way and under the right circumstances. After all, righteousness comes from God. His Word says that victory is mine.

The years passed. When I left home I ran scared hiding anywhere I could while my mother searched everywhere for me. Then one day she came to school giving her grand performance of a devotedly loving mother in search of her very confused daughter. The school office used the class-room intercom to announce their request "Ms. Alexander, please send Susan to the office." Fear struck, my heart raced and my body broke into a nervous sweat as I hesitantly crept up from my seat. Sad frightened eyes were fixed upon my teacher hoping to gain her attention long enough to send her a silent plea for help. Breathless and aware of my doom I continued my silent plea as if to say, "Please don't send me to the office." My teacher was so absorbed with her class that she quickly turned toward me with a smile to say goodbye. Then immediately she drew her attention back to the class completely unaware of my desperate plea for help. I slowly turned toward the open classroom door and quietly escaped down the empty hallway in search of a place to hide; an empty room, bathroom stall, even behind the shrubs on school grounds. Where should I go? Outside the building is where I felt the safest. I ran towards the woods on the edge of the school grounds and hid until the search was over. Then I left school for that day.

Finally three weeks of dodging my mother's fury had passed. Now eighteen, I was legally independent. I completed eleventh and twelfth grades and graduated high school with a college scholarship. Jesus Christ became my Lord and Savior. From that day on, I knew I was not alone and did not have to be afraid any longer. Over the course of time, Jesus made my dreams a reality and gave me the desires of my heart. Although I continued to overcome struggles in life, I learned not to carry my past on my shoulders. After completing college, I began a teaching career. It took the unconditional love of Jesus Christ, persistence, and a willful heart, mind, and soul for me to learn to love, let go of my past, and prepare for future challenges. I knew the road ahead would be difficult to travel having many challenges to overcome, but now I have help. Now I say, "Victory is mine. God loves me and I can do all things through Jesus Christ who saved me." Today I live my life in full-time ministry for Jesus Christ. I gained a true understanding of God's unconditional love and

was able to forgive my mother and father. Taking account-
ability for my future, I realized the choices for healthier
living are mine alone to make. I also learned to love through
Jesus Christ. The road traveled was not easy. The memories
linger. Sometimes my body still trembles as an automatic
response to a screaming child in a supermarket or anywhere.
Praying for that child always seems to help me to have
peace. I also remember three scriptures, *"Greater is he that
is in me than he that is in the world."* 1John 4:4. *"I can do
all things through Christ who strengthens me."* Philippians
4:13. *"With God all things are possible."* Matthew 19:26. Oh
yes, and one more, *"But thanks be to God, which giveth us
the victory through our Lord Jesus Christ."* 1 Corinthians
15:57.

You must take responsibility for your actions and your
attitude in order for change to begin in your life. How much
control do you have over your life? Do you still blame others
from your past for the life you live now? Change begins with
self. So stop making excuses for your present circumstances.
If God can see room for change and have hope in you, if God
does not look upon your sins, hold a grudge, and can forgive
you, then you, who are less than God, can forgive yourself
and others by letting go. Let go of your past. Let go of your
guilt and shame. No one knows of your prior life experiences unless you tell them to someone. Instead, give them
over to God who offers the opportunity for a new beginning

in life, a brand new start. God sees you as a winner and an over comer. You must see yourself the same way.

God's desire is for you to enjoy life right now one day at a time, not when all your conditions for healthy living are met, not when you have a happier marriage or a better job, not when your health or finances improve, not when you have a more reliable car or can take a vacation. Stop letting the time for joy pass you buy as if to wait for the right opportunity. Now is the time for change. Change begins when you allow it to happen and originates from within. Let's look at some key questions, which will help you to make changes in your life.

1. Do you speak openly your beliefs and views with others?
2. Does fear of rejection and lack of confidence control your ability to express yourself?
3. Are you aware of your gifts and talents given by God?
4. How do you use your gifts and talents?
5. Are you willing to live your life committed to God; putting aside society's standard for living?

Take the challenge and you will find that love is a life force empowered by self-will and a deep desire for fulfillment pleasing to God.

# The Fruit of Love

❧❦❧

G od desires fruit as in 1 Corinthians 13 where the fruit of love is expressed as kindness, joy, peace, long-suffering, patience, faithfulness, humbleness, selflessness, and being trustworthy. Love's fruit grows within those who have the mind of Jesus Christ. Fruit bearers then become rich in God's unconditional love. To become fruit bearers, you must become Godly minded results in having a pure heart, and a cleansed soul, which therefore, produces the fruit of love in all things. This outpouring of God's love in faith is what changes obstacles into opportunities, tragedies into triumphs, stumbling blocks into stepping-stones, and stress into strength. The more quality time you put into the things of God, the greater the return of blessings to you in your present life and in life eternal. As you make changes in your surroundings, the people you associate with, and strengthen your relationship with God, you will find true unconditional love. *"A new commandment I give to you, that you love one another, even as I have loved you, love one another."* John 13:34. *"God is love; and he that dwelleth in love dwelleth in God and God in him."* 1 John 4:16.

*"Beloved, let us love one another, for love is from God; and everyone that loveth is born of and knoweth God. He that loveth not knoweth not God, for God is love. In this was manifested the love of God toward us, because that God sent his only begotten Son into the world, that we might live through him. Herein is love, nor that we loved God, but that he loved us, and sent his Son to be the propitiation for our sins. Beloved, if God so loved us, we ought to love one another."* 1 John 4:7-11.

# *Love*

Love offers lessons in healthy living.

Love requires nothing in return.

Love does not pass judgment between right or wrong.

Love does not need to be rewarded

Love cannot be found in someone else.

Love creates its own energy from within.

Love is a driving force in human natures.

Love sustains itself with continual input to the soul.

Love is omnipresent.

God is love!

*By Susan DeRienzo*

# Love Makes a Difference

Love is not judgmental.
Love is not demanding.
Love breaks down barriers.
Love makes a difference.

Love requires sacrifice and commitment.
Love never assumes to know.
Love forgives.
Love makes a difference.

Love encourages.
Love builds trust.
Love wills itself to grow.
Love makes a difference.

Love is an act of faith.
Love is unconditional.
Love is a way of life.
Love makes a difference.
God is love!

*By Susan DeRienzo*

## Chapter 8

# Self-Discovery

❦

The Bible is full of inspiring scripture telling you to let yourself go, be who you are on the inside, give your vulnerabilities and insecurities to Jesus, and have confidence in your creator who knows you better than you do. However what if you don't know who you are on the inside or what your purpose for living is? Have you discovered your talents your abilities or your strengths and weaknesses? With the hustle and bustle this life brings, who has time to think? It's a jungle out there. You look back and say, "Where has the time gone?" You want to know your purpose for living. You want to make a difference in your life and in the lives of others. You want to contribute to society. Therefore, you ask yourself, "What can I do?" "Where do I begin?" "How do I get started?"

*First, you must find value in who you are*. Develop your self-worth. You can start by treating yourself the way you want to be treated by others. Show yourself the respect you know you deserve. Focus on loving yourself the way God loves you, unconditionally. Do not be so hard on yourself.

*Second, seek ways to develop gifts and talents.* Start by analyzing that which interests you most. Gifts and talents are sometimes hidden within daily routines. Look at where your personal interests lie. What do you enjoy doing most? Explore the reason why you enjoy what you do. Do you like to be around children? Are you a caregiver? Do you like to work with numbers or with your hands? Maybe you like to use reasoning skills or hold debates. Pay close attention to compliments received from others. However small and insignificant they may be to you, they may reveal a strong point you never knew you had.

*Third, trust your judgments.* Be assertive and true to you. Learn to be victorious in your quest for self-worth. Too often there are those who live their lives always being on guard and cautious. Those who hold back for fear of being taken advantage of. You guard your heart from risks of any kind. You are reluctant to try for fear of the consequences. Instead, boldly speak out about how you feel. Voice your opinions and your ideas. You may be nervous and shy at first but with each attempt made your confidence and boldness increases. Start with something easy and work your way up. I use to have this tormenting fear of talking on the phone to where my mind would go blank when the person I called would pick up and say, "Hello." I tried memorizing what I want to say on the phone but my mind would still go blank. I tried discussing my fear with others but that didn't work either. The problem was that I did not know where this fear came from. Therefore, the problem seemed to have no end. Determined to overcome my fear, one day I decided to write my thoughts down before making a call. Then I would read from my notes what I wanted to say. My stomach was in knots, my body would break out in a nervous sweat and my voice trembled but I was communicating with the person on the other end of the receiver. This lasted some time until one day, in gentleness and all sincerity, the man whom I was speaking to at the time told me that he could tell I was reading to him. I remember feeling the blood rush to my head as I turned beet red with embarrassment. However, I pressed on and God gave me the victory. Now I speak boldly and with confidence in front of large audiences, everywhere God sends me.

Finally, it is vitally important to learn the art of treating yourself to a few precious moments each day. Have you ever noticed that no matter how insanely busy your day may be you will always find time to go to the bathroom, get some sleep, eat a meal, or talk on the phone? Your body demands attention and won't let up until you respond. A full bladder, fatigue, hunger pains, and the need to hear another person's voice are signals from your body that tell you to STOP. Put yourself above your daily routine and hectic work schedule. If you don't your body will give you deficiency signals;

frustration, confusion, fatigue, lack of concentration, lack of motivation, depression, a full bladder, and sickness to name a few. Respect your well-deserved need for a break and if necessary find a replacement to cover for you. Take a vacation or some time off. Remember to observe the Sabbath as God did. Find that balance in your daily routine between your needs and the needs of others. You will not regret it.

Speaking of daily routines, have you ever asked yourself the following questions? How do I feel at this very moment? What do I need right now? If you feel happy and content then stay with what you are doing. If you feel unfulfilled frustrated and maybe even board then you need to make a change. Try a new method for accomplishing tasks, a new job, or maybe your own business, one that is more rewarding, fulfilling and more challenging. Experiment a little by making yourself more comfortable before starting a task, maybe a cup of tea, a warm sweater, a quick phone call to give you peace of mind, and always a prayer or two. I find that praying for others sometimes helps take the focus off my circumstances. Even if prayer is a temporary release, it is still an opportunity to be better prepared for tasks. In searching for a job or starting your own business, think beyond the obvious skills and present experience. A good change is to focus on what you enjoy in life not on what you think you have to do but on what you want to do.

Learning to love you is very challenging because most of what you think and do reflect others. You sacrifice self for the sake of others, a very sincere and noble task, but there needs to be a balance between self and others. If not, you will loose strength and momentum to continue. Things pile up and you feel weighed down. You may take a vacation only to come back to the same routine. Also, consider the power of your thoughts. Do you have control over your thoughts? Do you distinguish between negative and positive input to your mind? Do people who support your ideas surround you; those who encourage and strengthen you with good sound advice, and maybe even lend a helping hand? Or are you surrounded by contention, dysfunction, pressure, belittling, strife, and other negative influences? What fills your mind each day? What do you want to fill your mind? Do you have peace when you go to bed at night or are you relieved that you don't have to hear anymore? It is time to take control over your thoughts! Refuse to entertain negative talk. Do not subject yourself to sarcasm and ridicule or other people's problems. You know what I mean. You decide. Be an independent thinker. Walk away from negative influencing or intimidating conversations. The bathroom is a great escape where you can pray or go outside for a bit of fresh air. After all, people go outside to have a cigarette. Take authority over your life right now! Go outside or away from a negative situation, that does not involve you. There may even be someone else outside for the same reason. Surround yourself with positive minded people. Purposefully fill your mind with positive thinking. Self-help videos, tapes, DVD's and books are great resource materials. Pray continually and meditate on God's Word daily. This is your number one source of peace, comfort, and answered prayer. Many times our thoughts control our actions. Begin now by not letting anyone or any situation become an excuse for not setting yourself free. Get on the road to self-discovery. Do not look to the left or the right; just within. The past is no excuse because the past is over. The mind is no excuse because you can learn to control your thoughts. Others are no excuse because you have every right to choose who you want to associate with. If circumstances beyond your control surround you, remember to find your secret prayer closet and retreat to it as often as possible. Pray ask God for wisdom and help. You are not alone. God is always with you waiting for you to meet with him. Do not limit yourself now because of those who hurt you in your past. Open your heart and mind to forgiveness. You are not responsible for all your experiences so grow out of it and move on. God does not bring the thing forgiven back for future remembrance, you do. I speak to you from personal experience both as a child and in my adult life. It is by God's hand and his grace that I am alive today. Now the choice is yours. Love God. Love yourself; moreover, get on the road to freedom. Remember, you are never alone when you diligently ask and seek God for help.

*"For I know the thoughts that I think towards you, saith the Lord, thoughts of peace, and not of evil, to give you an expected end. And ye shall seek me, and find me, when ye*

*shall search for me with all your heart."* Jeremiah 29:11, 13. God calls for you to have faith in him. Expect God to finish the work he has begun in you. You will see deliverance come into your life as you seek God with all your heart.

*"God is our refuge and strength, a very present help in trouble."* Psalms 46:1. This Psalm was written to give encouragement and comfort in times of distress, to remind us that God triumphs over evil and in times of deep despair.

*I will instruct thee and teach thee in the way which thou shalt go; I will guide thee with mine eye."* Psalm 32:8. God blessed King David in writing a book of Psalms filled with instruction and counsel for living. This verse of scripture is an example of God providing spiritual guides and over-seers to help us through life. King David spoke this verse as a commitment to those who sat under his instruction. Just as God watches over us, he also sends spiritual leaders and counselors to do the same. Check to see that you are in a good Bible based church with loving and caring people of God, even if it means finding another church more suitable for spiritual growth.

*"Be still and know* [recognize and understand] *that I am God."* Psalms 46:10. God wants you to remember that his perfect will is at work in your life when you allow it to be. He gives you long lasting peace, security, and assurance when you put your trust in him exercising your faith through continual fervent prayer.

*"But my God shall supply all your need according to his riches in glory by Christ Jesus."* Philippians 4:19. Depend on God who meets all your needs. God is your supplier not this world. God's riches are found in those things that glorify him. By performing acts of kindness and generosity, by showing God's unconditional love to others with a willful heart, and by seeking God first in your life, then you are in accordance with God's will. Whether your need is spiritual or material God will supply your every need when you seek him first through Jesus Christ.

*"Jesus Christ is the same yesterday, and today, and forever."* Hebrews 13:8. The Bible clearly states that no matter how many different doctrines there are you must live each day by faith that never changes. You are to live by faith in Jesus Christ who also never changes.

*"Delight thyself also in the Lord; and he shall give thee the desires of thine heart."* Psalms 37:4. Love the things of God and live for him. Choose to live life by placing your confidence in God. Make God your first hope and he will give you comfort in this world. Trust in God not man. God gives many examples in His Word of how he will provide for you in this world because he gives you the desires of your heart. However, you must first delight in God, his will, his way, his glory by grace through Jesus Christ your Lord and Savior. Psalms 37:4 is not referring to the appetite of the flesh, but of your heart (soul). The soul desire of a good man or woman is to know God's love and live for God in a way

pleasing to him. God must be your guide through all affairs in life. Make it your privilege to delight in the Lord and he will give you the desires of your heart to full satisfaction. It is as His Word says, *"Give and it shall be given unto you."* Luke 6:38. Give to God and he will give back to you. Even in your poverty or mediocrity, you are to give to God, not just financially but also from your heart. Develop a heavenly account with God. Make deposits into your heavenly account through acts of selflessness, kindness, and generosity toward others as Christ did. Love and give with a willful heart and God who sees all will supply your needs more abundantly. Christ longs to give abundantly and wants to do so through you, his willing vessel. As you give to God, he will give back to you so you can share your wealth with others.

Co-labor with God. Work together with God. Sow seed and watch God make the seed grow. All you need to do is sow seeds of hope, kindness, compassion, love, patience, and financial blessing. All belongs to God who gave to you. Don't be afraid to let go of the little bit that you have. God is watching to see what you will do with the little he gives to you, to see how you will use it for his sake not your own. If you sow sparingly by trying to hold onto the little you have then you will reap sparingly because that is the amount you sowed. As in the *parable of the talents* found in Matthew 25:14-30, the man who was given one talent did not use it, therefore, the talent was taken from him and given to another who was not afraid to sow or invest it. You would think that those who are given more have more to lose and therefore would be more reluctant to invest for fear of losing much. The man with one talent feared having nothing and ended up with nothing. Have faith rather than fear. Share your home with others. Stretch out a meal to share with another. Give a child in your neighborhood or church a toy you know will put a smile on his or her face. Offer gas or food money to a needy person or family. Develop your heavenly account with God. Give back to God from what he has given to you and you will gain the favor of those around you and of God. You will have made investments into your heavenly account of good deeds that will not return void. God who sees and watches everything you do will give more to you because he knows you will give to others. He knows your heart and sees your good works. Moreover, remember to give first to God through your church. You do not want to make God jealous by giving to your family, relatives or close friends first as if they are more important than God. You do not want to chance giving to self and others and not have anything left to give to God who gave all to you to begin with. Make God your first priority. He has control over your heavenly account not you. The more you give the more God will give to you because of your generosity in Christ Jesus. Discover the *giver* in you and see what God will do because of his unconditional love for you. Share with others the love God placed inside of you when he created you. Be of good cheer and know that he is with you forever and ever.

*Chapter 9*

# Forgiveness from the Heart

⚜

Forgiveness means to pardon without holding a grudge. To let go of your anger especially when you do not want to, and to release your debtor from the debt owed. True forgiveness means you do not look back at what you have forgiven. Forgive with all your heart having no reservation of doubt.

You might say, Susan, "You don't know how much I've been hurt. You don't know the pain I've suffered or what I've been through over the years." This is true but the question is do you want to carry the weight of your grudge everywhere you go the rest of your life or release it? God did not intend for you to suffer. So let go of the grudge you have held on to for so long. I know it is not easy but its worse to let anger, bitterness, doubt, pain, or a sorrowful heart full of self-pity control your life. You have dominion and authority over your thoughts and your actions. You have the ability to choose to enjoy life or not to. You can focus on negativity resulting from your past or choose to focus on the positive. This doesn't mean to say, "Maybe someday I'll forgive; I just can't right now." I must tell you that there is no time like the present to release a grudge and to forgive. The past is over and the future is uncertain. The resent exists at this very moment. You can choose to make a difference in your life right now while reading this passage of my book.

Each dreaded step I took toward home from school my stomach was in knots for fear of not knowing what to expect from my mother. I always feared the worst as I wondered what fait awaited my arrival, chores or another beating. I felt alone in a great big world with lots of painful secrets. What choice did I have? Whom could I speak to? What if my mother found out I told someone? What would she do to me then? Who would believe me? Deep despair and fear of the unknown haunted my mind. I was panic stricken all the way home every day. Behind closed doors were secrets the outside world knew nothing about. I was a prisoner of doom with no escape except when on the wings of my imagination. Many times my thoughts would take me to a place where children played together in harmony and love, where kindred-spirited parents would train up their children preparing them for a future full of opportunity. Now you know the imagination can be a wonderful and safe place to hide. I am sure you go there from time to time like me. I went there quite often especially with a deep longing for my mother's love, a kind word, or a hug. Instead, I found myself watching the tender care that other mothers gave their children as the lyrics of a song about a motherless child lived in my heart. For years, the melody of this song played in my mind as I clung to a deep desire for that healthy mother-daughter relationship.

Now a teenager the lonely fearful walks home from school brought me closer to the day of my escape. Moreover, one day I did just that. I left home entering a world I knew nothing about but not before learning that my mother was diagnosed with "manic-depression and paranoid schizophrenia." In my mind, mental illness hindered my hope for her acceptance and approval.

I understand failure, words of destruction, abuse, suicidal attempts, and despair. Growing up all I thought about was living on my own away from the ritual beatings and constant ridicules. When my first attempt to run away failed, I tried again at age seventeen just three weeks before my eighteenth birthday. I hid from my mother's wrath until I turned eighteen. Living from house to house and being unwanted was very hard. Then one day I told Lori, a friend from school, about my situation. Lori told me about Jesus Christ; how much he loved me and wanted to help me. I knew I needed help. I never heard anything bad about Jesus, so I thought why not; I said the sinner's prayer with Lori and accepted Jesus Christ as my Lord and Savior. Next thing I knew, Terry, Lori's piano teacher wanted to meet me at her home. After explaining my reason for leaving home and seeing that

I genuinely was seeking a safe and healthy life, Terry and her family accepted me into their home to live. Terry was a nurse by profession. She gave me the medical care I needed and encouraged mc to go forward with my life. I completed high school and received a college scholarship from a local charitable organization. Jesus gave me the ability to go from a failing student to a "B" student, from despair to having hope, from being lost, insecure, and full of fear, to having a purpose, being loved, and told that I am of great value to God.

Over the next few years, I made weekly Sunday afternoon visits to see my mother. We would sit in the family room two to three hours with barely a word spoken. Each week her cold non-responsive deliberate stare away from me stirred up disappointment and a need to keep praying. After three years of weekly visits and no communication, I reduced my visits to twice a month. Even then, her anger and stubbornness prevailed. Eventually I stopped going home. I stopped trying so hard to make things work. Her stubborn rejection toward me was not mine to receive. I put my hope in Jesus Christ, chose to forgive my mother and earnestly continued praying. Then one day I realized that even though I forgave my mother I still carried anger towards her. I felt that I deserved a loving relationship and that she had no right to be angry with me for anything not even leaving home but she did remain very angry. She felt that I left her not home. Well, what did she expect? I had a choice to take the abuse or not to. I chose to protect myself and explore the unknown potentials life had to offer. I chose to reject negativity and believe that I would be better off outside my home. I made the right choice for me but was still empty on the inside. What could cause my mother to be so angry and bitter? If I only knew, what she was thinking. Then maybe we could have a loving mother-daughter relationship. Instead, I realized that my lack of understanding prevented me from truly forgiving my mother with a whole heart. I harbored anger deep inside my heart. Focused on being a victim I failed to observe her needs. I simply believed my mother was wrong about many things. However, it is not about whose right or wrong is it?

Forgiveness begins when you allow for change in your thinking. Many people live moody grumpy lives mistakenly believing that forgiveness must come from the one you are in disharmony with. That a person would rely on the forgiveness of others in order to set himself free. In reality, forgiveness comes from the ability to forgive you, therefore, releasing yourself to go forward in life. Apologize if necessary and move on hoping the other person receives your forgiveness. Pray for the situation at hand. However, do not think that you have to do all you can to fix the problem. Do not feel guilty if the other person holds a grudge. After all, it is his or her grudge to hold not yours. Let him hold it if he wants to. Just set yourself free to move on. Also, be sensitive to the circumstances of others. Some people's inability to forgive you may be related to a completely different set of circumstances having nothing to do with you, as in the case with my mother. I visited my mother repeatedly hoping for a change. Change never came. I had to choose between clinging to my pain or releasing it; holding a grudge or letting it go, receiving her deliberate silent treatments or rejecting them.

There are situations in life we cannot control. Let go and let God is what we are taught. Therefore, I chose to let go of the situation with my mother. I stopped trying so hard. I went on with my life keeping hope in my heart. There was now no communication between us at all. Several years later, I made one more attempt to communicate with my mother by sending her a letter. She called me three weeks later. We talked about some questions I wrote in the letter mainly asking why, why for many things. My mother was angry and defensive when she said, "You deserved everything you got!" After so many years of hopelessness, I became so angry that I shouted, "NOBODY DESERVES TO GET HIT WITH A TWO BY FOUR, especially a child!" My heart sunk to the pit of my stomach at her cold unsympathetic response. Tears, sadness, and anger resurfaced. I thought, "How could she be so cruel?" We talked a little longer to no prevail. Not being able to listen to any more rejection, I hung up on her. All I wanted to do now was bury my disappointments for good and accept my fate of feeling like a motherless child. However, I was glad my mother responded to my letter even if it was hurtful because we communicated. Maybe my mother was glad to receive my letter. Maybe she called because she too had a glimmer of hope for us. My mother's attempt for a relationship became evident years later.

Two hours before Hurricane Katrina hit our Mississippi Gulf Coast home, I drove my family northwest to a church we had visited for the first time that same morning, a three-hour journey to safety. We stayed two weeks in a Sunday school classroom before driving on to a five-week stay at my sister's home in Canada. This is where I learned that my mother would not believe I was alive until she could hear my voice on the telephone. One time my sister, Sandi, attempted to hand me the phone saying that my mother wanted to talk to me. My heart sunk to the pit of my stomach. Anger rose up inside of me as I said, "You tell mom that I am fine." A few days later Sandi handed me the phone saying, "Someone wants to talk to you." Taking the phone and recognizing that it was my unsympathetic mother, I held nothing back. I released a lot of anger that day. I told my mother exactly how I felt, that I did not deserve the beatings or the neglect. I told her how convinced I was that she hated me. I even gave her a list of reasons why. However, this phone conversation was different. All my mother kept saying was that she was sorry. She kept asking for my forgiveness. Now that I was opening up and releasing my true feelings, I refused to hear her apologies and ignored her request for my forgiveness. I just poured into her all my bottled up anger and frustrations all my thoughts and feelings. Then I began to feel something happening as if a heavy weight lifted from within me. In addition, my mother just kept saying how sorry she was. There were no hurtful words or expressions of anger from her. She just kept apologizing and stayed calm. God was using hurricane Katrina, my sister, and my mother's frail condition to mend the broken heartedness between us. Even then, I still vented with everything in me because now I had another reason to be angry. My mother knew she was dying and wanted to make amends now at the end of her life. I felt cheated and outraged. What about the life we could have had together? Why wait until now? My mother is leaving soon and my prayers still unanswered. However, I knew my attitude was not helping the situation. Therefore, I took a deep breath thought more of her weakened condition and accepted her forgiveness. I said to my mother that I forgive her and asked for her forgiveness in return. This time I forgave my mother with my whole heart. This meant I had to be willing to open my heart to receive her forgiveness even after all that has happened between us. I chose to let go of the past and the pain she caused, therefore, allowing room in my heart for my mother's forgiveness. The seed of forgiveness was now planted in both of us. This phone conversation was the beginning of a much-needed healing process.

After five weeks in Canada, it was time to go home. We drove back to Mississippi with a U-haul full of blessings. My new hope was that maybe my mother would have a few special words to say to me before she died. Several months later, I was surprised when I received mail from my mother. She sent me my first birthday card from her in many years. I was delighted to find a beautiful gold charmed cross necklace taped to the inside of my birthday card. A short time later, I received a call from my sister saying that my mother was near her time. I flew to Arizona where my mother lived, still hoping for those special words just for me, her oldest daughter. Upstairs in her bedroom I sat on the chair by her bed and prayed, "Lord, I may only have one chance to hear my mother say anything. Do I ask about me or do I ask about you?" I knew the answer but the anguish of not hearing those special words overwhelmed me. Therefore, I slowly leaned closer to my mother and said in a gentle whisper, "Mom, I'm here, it's Susan." Her eyes began moving as if in a dream state. I said again, "Mom, its Susan." Her sunken eyes slowly opened. She sluggishly turned her head toward me, smiled, and said, "I'm ready to go home." Then she gradually turned her head back to its original position and closed her eyes to sleep. Sitting by her bedside I looked around the room until my eyes became fixed on the opened Bible resting on a table at the foot of her bed. I picked it up noticing all her pen marks, underlines, and noted in the margins. My mother spent many long days and nights with Jesus. Her words to me were the last I received from her before she died. I had peace for my mother knowing she died in peace with Jesus Christ.

Later I learned that the beautiful charmed necklace was one of four necklaces she purchased, one for each of her daughters. My mother made sure that I received mine directly from her to me. I can picture my mother very carefully selecting this necklace at the department store. The effort she must have exerted to make the drive to the post office to mail my gift. I believe my mother knew that this would be very meaningful to me. In addition, those few special words I longed to hear her say were written in the card my mother sent me. She wrote those special words so I could see it with my own eyes, and always remember. *"I Love You, Mom"*. My mother died in peace and my prayer answered in the best way my mother knew how. Though she did not speak the words, she wrote them for me to cherish always.

You see, it was wrong of me to ask something from someone who could not give the thing asked for. It is like praying for someone else's salvation. You can pray and pray but your prayers will not save a person. It is up to the unsaved person to want salvation. That is the beauty of God's free will. In the same way that a person must receive salvation through Jesus Christ in order to be saved, my mother needed to first receive God's unconditional love in order to have unconditional love in her to give. She knew God's love existed but maybe didn't know how to receive and use God's love in order to share God's love with others. The point is that my mother was hurting too. She suffered severely in her own life as a child and later as an adult. By age seventeen, she left home for marriage. The next thing she knew, she was a single mom on welfare with five small children. All her future hopes and dreams were shattered. She tried to be strong but her mind got the best of her and wore her out. My mother needed help; a personal relationship with Jesus Christ. Instead, her children received the repercussion of her anger and frustration. It was my mother who first needed to receive love in order to give love. Now in writing this chapter I realize more than ever before that my mother and I were both hurting and suffering over the same thing; a lack of love. I learned to forgive all the beatings, the loneliness, destructive words, and mental anguish I held on to for so long. Maybe my mother did not know how to release her pain and anguish unto Jesus. She knew and believed in Jesus but did not have a personal relationship with him as her Savior until her life was ending. Daily she began reading and studying God's Word. She began seeking forgiveness from those she hurt. In the end, my mother allowed Jesus to be Lord of her life. I believe our relationship would have been different. Nevertheless, what is truly important is that we forgave each other.

You will experience pain in life but you do not have to keep suffering for it. Do not allow your life to become paralyzed by misfortune. Forgiveness is not easy but it is essential for peace and harmony in life. The more you forgive the less room there will be in your heart for guilt, anger, and despair. By allowing for sincere forgiveness, your heart will be full of joy. Your mind will think more clearly and you will view life from a healthier and more spiritual perspective. Be encouraged. God wants to plant seeds of forgiveness, hope, and opportunity into your heart. The more you open your heart to him the more you allow God to do a work in you. Forgiveness takes an act of your will to forgive others and to be forgiven. Will you open your heart to forgiveness today? *"Forgiveness comes from God."* Nehemiah 9:17.

*"And be ye kind one to another, tenderhearted, forgiving one another, even as God for Christ's sake hath forgiven you."* Ephesians 4:32.

## Chapter 10

# God's Healing Power

❧✥☙

*"Surely he hath born our griefs, and carried our sorrows;*
*yet we did esteem him stricken, smitten of God, and afflicted.*
*But he was wounded for our transgressions; he was bruised*
*for our iniquities: the chastisement of our peace was upon*
*him; and with his stripes, we are healed. All we like sheep*
*have gone astray; we have turned everyone to his own way;*
*and the Lord hath laid on him the iniquity of us all."* Isaiah
53:4-6.

Jesus obeyed his Father even unto death in the cross. He
willingly bore your griefs and carried your sorrows, per-
severed through all manner of evil, endured severe scourging,
scandal, and slander in order to set you free from sin. Jesus'
heart ached for you with great compassion as if to say Father
not my will but thy will be done. When Jesus died, he went
to save and heal you from all your iniquities. His body,

soul, and spirit went to set free your body, soul, and spirit from Satan's grasp, therefore, making redemption for you complete spiritually and physically. When Jesus said, "It is finished," he knew his suffering was made complete. The commandment of the Father was fulfilled for you to be spiritually and physically set free. All Old Testament prophecies of the Messiah's sufferings were accomplished. The laws of Moses were fulfilled that you may live by faith. Although Jesus had the wisdom and the power to evade the cross, he chose to submit his body, soul, and spirit to the cross for your sins. "It is finished," means that an end has come for all sin.

*"Behold the Lamb of God, which taketh away the sin of the world."* John 1:29.

Spiritually through Jesus Christ, you are saved. Physically through Jesus Christ, you are healed. Nothing was left undone. The atonement Jesus made was for the deliverance of sin and sickness. The soul was delivered from sin. The body was delivered from sickness. Jesus recognized the body as well as the soul. Sin and sickness are equally important to God. If only half your being was delivered then you would not be made whole. God is the Savior of the body and the soul for all humanity.

*"...God is no respecter of persons,"* Acts 10:34.

106

God does not choose who is to be or not to be healed. It is God's will that all be healed and healed through the atonement of Jesus Christ. The most powerful manifestation of God is in the arena of healing. Healing the sick drew large crowds then and still does today. Spiritual and physical healing is a part of the greatest expressions of God's unconditional love to his children.

*"And Jesus went about all the cities and villages, teaching in their synagogues, and preaching the gospel of the kingdom, and healing every sickness and every disease among the people." Matthew 9:35.*

*"And Jesus went about all Galilee, teaching in their synagogues, and preaching the gospel of the kingdom, and healing all manner of sickness and all manner of disease among the people. And his fame went throughout all Syria: and they brought unto him all sick people that were taken with divers diseases, and torments, and those which were possessed with devils, and those which were lunatic, and those that had the palsy; and he healed them. And there followed him great multitudes of people from Galilee, and from Decapolis, and from Jerusalem, and from Judea and from beyond Jordan."* Matthew 4:23-25.

*"...And many followed him, and he healed them all."* Matthew 12:15.

*"When Jesus heard of it,* [the death and burial of John the Baptist], *he departed thence by ship into a desert place apart: by himself; and when the people had heard thereof, they followed him on foot out of the cities. And Jesus went forth, and saw a great multitude, and was moved with compassion toward them, and he healed their sick."* Matthew 14: 13-14.

*"And he arose out of the synagogue, and entered into Simon's house. And Simon's wife's mother was taken with a great fever; and they besought him for her. And he stood over her, and rebuked the fever; and it left her: and immediately she arose and ministered unto them. Now when the sun was setting, all they that had any sick with divers' diseases brought them into him; and he laid his hands on every one of them, and healed them. And devils also came out of many, crying out, and saying, "Thou are Christ the Son of God;" And he rebuking them suffered them not to speak: for they knew that he was the Christ. And when it was day, he departed and went into a desert place: and the people sought him and came unto him, and stayed with him, that he should not depart from them."* Luke 4:38-43.

Jesus performed the works of God on earth as a sign of who he was. It was a performance to help people to believe that God sent him. It was not until Calvary that Jesus took upon himself the sins of the world to save you and set you free from sickness and disease. God's will is for your bodies to be healed. When you break a bone, the cells in your body immediately begin a healing process. As soon as sickness enters your body, antibodies are on the scene fighting against germs and bacteria. God even heals cuts, bruises, and scrapes.

*"And as they departed from Jericho, a great multitude followed him. And, behold, two blind men sitting by the way side, when they heard that Jesus passed by, cried out saying, have mercy on us, O Lord, thou Son of David. And the multitude rebuked them, because they should hold their peace: but they cried out more, saying, Have mercy on us, O Lord, thou Son of David. And Jesus stood still, called them, and said, "What will ye that I should do unto you?" They said unto him, "Lord, that our eyes may be opened." And so Jesus had compassion on them, and touched their eyes: and immediately their eyes received sight, and they followed him."* Matthew 20:29-34.

*"And a certain woman which had an issue of blood twelve years, and had suffered many things of many physicians, and had spent all that she had, and was nothing bettered, but rather grew worse, when she had heard of Jesus, came in the press behind, and touched his garment. For she said, "If I may touch but his clothes, I shall be whole." And straightway the fountain of her blood was dried up; and she felt in her*

*body that she was healed of that plague. And Jesus, immediately knowing in himself that virtue had gone out of him, turned him about in the press, and said, "Who touched my clothes?" And his disciples said unto him, Thou seeth the multitude thronging thee, and sayest thou, who touched me? He looked around about to see her that had done this thing. But the woman fearing and trembling knowing what was done in her, came and fell down before him, and told him all the truth. And he said unto her, "Daughter, thy faith hath made thee whole; go in peace, and be whole of thy plague."* Mark 5:25-34.

*"He said unto them, "Peace; for the maid is not dead, but sleepeth." And they laughed him to scorn. But when the people were put forth, he went in, and took her by the hand, and the maid arose."* Matthew 9:24-26.

*But when he saw the multitudes, he was moved with compassion on them, because they fainted, and were scattered abroad, as sheep having no shepherd. Then saith he unto his disciples, the harvest truly is plenteous, but the laborers are few; pray ye therefore the Lord of the harvest that he will send forth laborers into his harvest."* Matthew 9:36-38.

Jesus was talking to his disciples about the tremendous amount of good works still needing to be done and that there were not enough workers to gather in the harvest. Many who were seeking salvation and deliverance needed God's Word and encouragement. The crowds that had gathered were becoming so large that Jesus commissioned his disciples for help. Like a farmer whose crops are ready to be harvested; but the laborers were few so the farmer goes out and finds more workers; those who are willing to gather in the harvest. Jesus, seeing the great work before him, *"called his twelve disciples together, and gave them power and authority over all devils, and to cure diseases. And he sent them to preach the kingdom of God, and to heal the sick."* Luke 9:1-2. *"And as ye go, preach, saying, the kingdom of heaven is at hand. Heal the sick, cleanse the lepers, raise the dead, cast out devils; freely ye have received freely give."* Matthew 10:7-8.

Jesus was not omnipresent during the time he walked on earth. He could only be in one place at one time. He needed help from his disciples. Therefore, he gave the disciples authority and empowered them with the ability to perform miracles; that others may believe in the One who sent them. This was the great commission set upon them; preach the gospel of Salvation and perform miracles in his name that the body may be saved as well as the soul. The disciples went abroad in every direction preaching the gospel, healing the sick, and casting out demons in the name of Jesus the Christ. Now there was a man with a son who appeared to have a mental illness that caused seizures and uncontrollable fits. After many disappointing results from physicians, the father brought his son to the disciples to be healed. The disciples failed to heal the father's son. The distressed father then brought his son directly to Jesus saying that Jesus' own disciples were not able to heal his son. Jesus' anger rose against the unbelieving crowd. He reproved those around him, except the disciples, because of their doubt and unbelief. Jesus cannot perform miracles when unfaithfulness resides in the hearts of those around him. Satan will seek every way possible to control the flesh in an attempt to weaken the spirit towards the ultimate destruction of the soul. The crowd's unbelief is what caused the disciple's faith to weaken, therefore resulting in their failure to heal the boy. This is a prime example allowed by God to teach and remind us that all is through Christ alone. Christ alone waves and delivers the oppressed. Jesus' response to the father was, *"If thou canst believe, all things are possible to him who believeth."* Mark 9:23. The father's unbelief, caused by numerous failed attempts in the past, now has turned to belief in Jesus Christ and the work he does. Jesus seeing the gathering of the crowd set the boy free from Satan's grasp by rebuking Satan with authority. Jesus set the boy's mind right to complete the healing. Satan has no power over Christ and is therefore defeated. No matter how long he resided in the boy, Satan must stand down to the power and authority of Jesus Christ. Jesus then commissioned the disciples saying that when they go out to do God's work they must also devote quality time with him. It is important to have a little

breathing time and mental rest, a time of solitude and medi-
tation with Jesus to replenish the mind, body, and spirit to go
out again. Christ then explains that their failure to heal was
caused by the unbelieving crowd. Weakened faith is ineffec-
tual. In a case like this, it is common for the lack of healing
to be blamed on ministers who then blame the crowd yet it
actually was both. He continues to say that it takes the faith
of a mustard seed grain to perform wonders for the glory
of God. So keep your faith active and growing continually.
Spend quality time meditating on scriptures and the things of
God. See Matthew 17:14 -21.

The news of Jesus was rapidly spreading in every direction through the work of his disciples. The harvest continued
to multiply greatly. Jesus had large crowds of people following him daily. Some in need of instruction others healing.
His work was continually increasing. Therefore, Jesus chose
seventy more from the crowd to send out two by two ahead
of him saying, *"the harvest truly is great, but the laborers
are few: pray ye therefore the Lord of the harvest, that he
would send forth laborers into his harvest. Go your ways:
behold, I send you forth as lambs among wolves."* Jesus sent
the seventy on ahead to preach the gospel and heal the sick.
Later, the seventy returned filled with joy and excitement
saying to Jesus, *"Lord, even the devils are subject unto us
through thy name."* Jesus replied, *"Behold, I give unto you
power to tread on serpents and scorpions, and over all the*

*power of the enemy and nothing shall by any means hurt you."* Luke 10:1-20.

God has such great compassion that he sent his Son. His Son has such great compassion for us that he sent his disciples and many others. God's great plan of salvation is for all to be set free from hell, sickness, and disease of every kind. Therefore, Jesus instructed his disciples saying, *"Go ye therefore, and teach all the nations, baptizing them in the name of the Father and of the Son, and of the Holy Ghost: teaching them to observe all things whatsoever I have commanded you: and lo, I am with you always, even to the end of the world."* Matthew 28:19-20. *"And he said unto them, go ye into all the world, and preach the gospel to every creature. He that believeth and is baptized shall be saved; but he that believeth not shall be condemned. And these signs shall follow him that believeth; in my name shall they cast out devils; they shall speak with new tongues; they shall take up serpents; and if they drink any deadly thing, it shall not hurt them; they shall lay hands on the sick, and they shall recover."* Mark 16:15-18.

Even the Gentiles will cast out demons, speak in tongues, be protected by God, and heal the sick. The mission of Jesus, originally intended for the Jewish nation, became available to all nations throughout the world. Remember, God is no respecter of persons. See the example found in Acts where God sent Peter, a Jew, into the home of Cornelius, a gentile, to preach to his entire household. *"While Peter yet spoke these words, the Holy Ghost fell on all them which heard the Word. And they of the circumcision, which believed, were astonished, as many as came with Peter, because that in the Gentiles also was poured out the gift of the Holy Ghost. For they heard them speak with tongues, and magnify God. Then answered Peter, can any man forbid water, that these would not be baptized, which have received the Holy Ghost as well as we? And he commanded them to be baptized in the name of the Lord. Then prayed they him to tarry certain days."* Acts 10:44-48.

God sent Jesus, Jesus sent his disciples and many others who went forth into all the land throughout all the earth to the end of the world. Three days after Jesus died; he resurrected and showed himself to the disciples. *"He breathed on them and saith unto them, receive ye the Holy Ghost."* John 20:22. Jesus showed the disciples that he was physically alive by breathing on them. He breathed the breath of life revealing himself as the author of life. Just as God breathed the breath of life into Adam, Jesus breathed life into his disciples making them ready to receive one of the most precious gifts of all, the Holy Spirit. He was sending them out letting them know that his Holy and precious Spirit will be with them always. He spoke over his disciples telling them of the coming of the Holy Spirit, a comforter and helper for them when Jesus ascends to heaven. *"Nevertheless I tell you the truth; it is expedient for you that I go away: for if I go not away, the **Comforter** will not come unto you; but if I* *depart, I will send him unto you. And when he is come, he will reprove the world of sin, and of righteousness, and of judgment...Howbeit when he, the **Spirit of truth**, is come, he will guide you into all truth,,," John 16: 7-15.*

Jesus paid a price for you. The fruit of that price is the Holy Spirit. Jesus said that he must ascend in order for the Comforter, the Holy Spirit, to descend upon his disciples and therefore upon all his children including you. Like babies weaned from their mother's milk the disciples needed to be weaned from the physical presence of Jesus Christ. His physical presence was continually looked upon and sought after through the eyes of man. The heart of a Godly man continually seeks the Spirit of God. Jesus taught his disciples that the kingdom he spoke of was spiritual not physical. He gave his disciples more knowledge than those in his presence, instruction sufficient to perform their duties, signs of future events, and a hope beyond all measure. The disciples were eager for knowledge. They were impatient for a new kingdom especially after they were told they would have a place of honor with the King in his kingdom. The disciples were given their tasks the authority to complete them and the assurance of their success in it. However, it would not be until they receive the baptism of the Holy Spirit that they truly would understand God's plan. So the disciples were instructed not to leave Jerusalem; that in a few days they will receive the Holy Spirit as God promised. Jesus reminded them of what John the Baptist spoke saying that he baptized with water but one is coming who will baptize you with the Holy Spirit, Mark 1:8. Jesus was explaining that his disciples would become supernaturally endowed with power from above. In addition, Jesus again made final mention of the disciples being his witnesses having a great commission to go and minister salvation and healing throughout the earth. He blessed them and ascended to Heaven.

After Jesus ascended, the disciples became apostles of Jesus Christ. Now that their instruction was complete, they were no longer as students with an instructor in a training program. The disciples became scholars full of knowledge and authority to go forth into all the earth preaching the gospel and healing the sick in the name of Jesus Christ of Nazareth; making them apostles, known as missionaries, evangelists, ministers, faith healers, teachers, and messengers of God. Their great commission would begin on the day of Pentecost, the seventh Sunday after the resurrection of Jesus Christ. The apostles assembled at Peter's house to pray. *"And suddenly there came a sound from heaven as of a rushing mighty wind, and it filled all the house where they were sitting. And there appeared unto them cloven tongues of fire, and it sat upon each of them. And they were all filled with the Holy Ghost, and began to speak with other tongues, as the Spirit gave them utterance."* Acts 2:2-4. Upon hearing this noise, a crowd of people gathered outside at Peter's house. As the apostles went outside the house, the multitude gathered around perplexed at what they were hearing from the mouths of the Galatians. The multitude was, in their hearing, receiving God's message to them in their native language. They questioned how these Galatians could be speaking in other native tongues. Some said that it was God. Others said that they were drunk with wine. Peter drew the attention of the crowd explaining, that which was foretold of this day by the prophets. He preached God's plan of salvation to the multitude. About three thousand souls were saved that day.

Peter and John continued their ministry in Jerusalem, daily preaching and teaching that Jesus is the Christ, and healing the sick in Jesus name. The number of disciples was increasing daily. Even Gentiles became disciples for Jesus Christ. See Acts chapter 10 and chapter 13:46-52. In addition to the increase in the number of disciples, many healings and miracles took place. The Apostle Peter's ministry grew. *"Insomuch that they brought forth the sick into the streets, and laid them on beds and couches, that at the least the shadow of Peter passing by might overshadow some of them. There came also a multitude out of the cities roundabout into Jerusalem, bringing sick folks, and them which were vexed with unclean spirits: and they were healed everyone."* Acts 5:15-16. The lame walked, the possessed were set free, the dead brought back to life, and many other miracles took place through truly devoted men and women of God who believed by faith in the power and authority given to them by God through Jesus Christ. The point is this; God, through his Son, has given you the opportunity to receive this same power and authority. God gave to his Son, who gave to his disciples, and to all of us throughout the entire world to the end of age. This means you too! Look, doubt can fill your mind if you let it, but facts are facts. Look at the following scriptures.

*"And he said unto them, go ye into all the world, and preach the gospel to every creature. He that believeth and is baptized shall be saved; but he that believeth not shall be condemned. And these signs shall follow him that believeth;* **in my name** *shall they cast out devils; they shall speak with new tongues; they shall take up serpents; and if they drink any deadly thing, it shall not hurt them; they shall lay hands on the sick, and they shall recover."* Mark 16:15-18.

*"Verily, verily, I say unto you, He* [all] *that believeth in me, the works that I do shall he do also; and greater works than these shall he do; because I go unto my Father."* John 14:12.

## Chapter 11

# Get Ready For a New Beginning

❧❦❧

Christian radio stations and television broadcasts share many exciting true stories of God's miracle working power. Incurable diseases disappear, tumors shrink to nothing, the paralytic walk, the deaf hear, the blind see, and the dumb speak. Then there are financial miracles, family members reunited, and the lost in Christ are found. These and many other miracles are taking place around the world at this very moment. The reason is because of people like you and me, believers who trust in God and allow themselves to be used to help make a difference in the lives of others.

To trust in God you must first stop looking at what you see in the mirror! Instead, see yourself through God's eyes of faith. God sees you the way he created you; full of potential and possibilities beyond your own understanding. God does not look at the natural man nor does he need the talents or abilities he gave you in order to accomplish his will in you. You have talents and abilities given to you by God to help you in this life until his Son returns. Use your gifts in a way that glorifies God. All God is looking for is a willful heart and a trusting soul. One who seeks his will and trusts in him totally. God needs people who look beyond the abilities of natural man into the possibilities of a supernatural God, people who do not rely on self but completely on God. You see, God can and will use anyone who is willing to be used of him. If you long to be used by God in a mighty way, then this chapter is for you.

Let's look at the following two questions. Why is it that when I ask God for help nothing happens? How can I bless others when I have not learned how to bless myself? If you are asking yourself these questions then you are on the right track. God clearly instructs us to *"ask, and it shall be given you; seek and ye shall find; knock, and it shall be open unto you."* Matthew 7:7. You have now taken the first step in asking God for answers. The next step is to research the things of God to gain wisdom, knowledge, and understanding. Read and study God's Word. If you find your Bible to be difficult to understand there are very well known anointed men and women of God who have completed extensive studies in God's Word and have written research materials to help you. Some of these materials are in the form of books, CD's, DVD's, and study Bibles. You will receive answered prayer through God's Word. Years are spent in college to master a profession. You invest time and money in How to…books, tools and supplies to develop skills and hobbies. A builder draws blueprints and computes many calculations before erecting a building. A farmer plows and cultivates his land before planting seed. The point is this, if you are willing to spend large amounts of time involved in the things of this world, then why not spend more time in the things of God who gave you life to begin with. Learn what it means to be a true believer of God. Read and study God's Word. Learn how to put your faith into action. The Bible gives many accounts of those who already reaped their blessings because of acting on their faith in God. Allow your faith in God to work for you too. Go for it! Increase your focus on the things of God and he will increase your understanding. Study your Bible. Start by taking the necessary steps to have good quality time with your creator. All he wants to do is bless you. So do your part expecting God to do his. The farmer who planted seed into the ground expects to reap a harvest. There is no doubt in his mind. He believes he will yield a harvest. He does not return to his seed and dig them up to see if they are germinating. Nor will the farmer pull out his young crop to see if it is taking root and then place it back into the ground. Instead, the farmer waits patiently for the harvest believing by faith for the fruit of all his hard work.

Just as a farmer labors to prepare his soil and a builder calculates to develop his blueprints, a child of God must dedicate quality time to the understanding of God's Word. *"Study to show thyself approved unto God."* 2 Timothy 2:15.

Persevere through the difficult parts of the Bible. Remember, God gives the understanding. Use reference materials to aid in your studies. Moreover, if you still do not understand something written in your Bible it's ok. What is equally important is that you have a willful heart towards God. Spend daily quality time developing a closer relationship with him. Include God in every part of your day. Believe by faith for the harvest of the blessings and miracles of God in your life. One day God may give you the understanding of that difficult passage of scripture when you least expect it. Continue to study and believe by faith. Take your mind off the business of your day. Become God-minded rather than self-minded. As you do this, the things you made a priority over God before now become secondary and you are blessed even more than before. Just say to yourself, *"I can do all things through Christ which strengtheneth me."* Philippians 4:13. When you expand your thinking to God's way of thinking the possibilities for spiritual growth are endless and far beyond your imagination. You will experience joy, peace, increased confidence, and self-worth. You will see yourself beautifully and wonderfully made. The excitement you experience in Christ will radiate through you onto others around you. In addition, remember God does not rely on how much experience you have, your level of education, your race, or how much money you have in order for him to use you. He is a God of the impossible. So expect God to give you a better life filled with new opportunities. Expect

God to bless you abundantly to where you can bless others. It's up to YOU. You will receive from life what you sow into it. So expect to reap your harvest now in this life. If you (sow) speak negatively and associate with negative minded people then you will reap a negative-minded lifestyle; one filled with doubt, hopelessness, poverty, and despair. If you (sow) speak positively and associate with positive minded people then you will reap the benefits and support of a positive minded lifestyle; you will have peace and abundant blessings. Surround yourself with people who encourage and build you up to be the best child of God you can. Expect to rise above your circumstances. Believe God for a productive rewarding future. Keep believing God by acting upon your will to believe. Put your faith into action. Prepare for your answered prayer. Be ready to receive from God. Maintain a consistent positive attitude. Read God's Word daily and study the scriptures. Fill your mind with the things of God. Choose a Bible topic of interest and research it. As you research, you grow in knowledge and grace. You will begin to see through spiritual eyes the things of God. It is like taking a walk and choosing to look down at the ground or to look up toward the heavens. Surround yourself with people who encourage you. The Bible says that if you stay with the wise, you become wise and if you stay with fools, you become foolish. Be sure to do all you can to live a right life with God and watch in amazement what he will do for you.

Believe God has more for you than you can imagine. He created you and knows everything about you. He sees many abilities deep inside you that you may not see in yourself. Little by little, the pressure and demands of life push strengths, talents, and creative abilities into the depths of your inner being. They are stored in a little compartment called a brain cell. From time to time, you reminisce until you say, "If only I..." or "I wish I...." Daily responsibilities and obligations took hold of you. They have become obstacles, trials, and stumbling blocks causing weakness in your character and in your ability to achieve your dreams. You live to survive. Your dreams, hopes, and aspirations seem like they will never come true. However, God doesn't see your life the way you do. He sees you for the potential he gave you to succeed and have peace. You may have made some mistakes along life's journey, but God sees and knows this and still believes in you for change. He believes you can make a difference in your own life. Challenge yourself believing in God for your dreams. Don't let fear of something new and different control your actions. Just take a step in faith. Watch and see what God will do for you. God works in mysterious ways, some more mysterious than others. Remember, he sees you for who he created you to be. You're just caught up in the jungle of life. All you have to do is believe in God's unconditional love, grace, and mercy for you and he will cause you to soar above all situations that come your way. The higher you soar, the further you will be from all that distracts you from following your dreams and the closer you will be to God. You have to stand tall to rise. God is the victor. Jesus said, *"I am the way, the truth, and the life..."* John 14:6. God can give you a dream and make your dream come true. All you need to do is listen to him and obey. Hear that whisper of a still small voice and challenge yourself to achieve your goals. Remember not to limit yourself. God does not need your money or education to accomplish his plan for you. He needs your willingness, faithfulness, and obedience. God is not limited by your thinking or by what you believe. So let go of self and let God enter in. Your lack of faith limits you. Do not settle for less, when God wants to give you more. Read your Bible. Study! Study! Study! Do not be concerned with what you don't understand. Just put into action the little you do understand. Use what you have learned and God will give you the increase. Put your trust completely in him. Don't think so much about the "what if's." You need to say to yourself, "Enough! I have had enough! I am not limiting myself anymore. I am entitled to more from God. I can do better and be a better child of God. I will learn to use the gifts God gave me to rise up and soar like an eagle. I will learn to soar because I am worth it. I am a child of the most high God who says that I deserve his best. I believe it and receive it today, right here, and right now, in Jesus precious and holy name, Amen."

Make room in your life for the manifestations of God. Get ready for a new beginning full of truth and amazement.

Watch what God will do for you as you let him. Think positive, be encouraged and go forth in the mane of Jesus Christ
of Nazareth. Let go of your past. Maintain a positive attitude. Let go of the pain, replacing it with joy and peace.
God sees all you have gone through in your past, where you
are right now, and he does not want you to limit him. God's
favor and unconditional love is yours. Take a stand in your
life to maximize your potential. Believe God will cause you
to be in the right place at the right time speaking to the right
person; a God connection to help you get to the next level of
achievement in your life. God wants to have a relationship
with you. He wants to move mountains in your life. God has
chosen you to be his instrument. He has already given you
his favor. God crowned you with his glory and his honor.
For you to receive and live in God's favor you must let go of
your life and give it back to God. Let God lead your life, the
life he gave you from the beginning.

There was a time when my husband was in the hospital
for nine weeks. Every evening I drove from work to visit him
before the long exhausting drive home. In addition, for some
reason I had been feeling unusually weak, almost faint at
times. Right from the start, I knew I needed God's favor for
a parking space and supernatural strength. I prayed without
having an ounce of doubt in my heart. I was desperate for his
help and knew the principle of not having doubt in my heart
or my mind. God's answer to me was a parking space close
to the hospital entrance for sixty-three consecutive days, the

full amount of time my husband was in the hospital. During this time, I visited my doctor who said my iron count was low do to stress. He suggested a few days off from work and an iron prescription. A year later and still having the same symptoms, tests revealed that a hemorrhage was causing the low iron count. Surgery was necessary. I asked God for his favor and he gave it to me. My husband and I are in good health today. The answered prayers were but a tiny measure of God's favor. Nothing we ask is insignificant to God not even a parking space.

God offers his favor to you simply by asking for it. There is no particular method or qualifications needed to receive God's favor. God does not look at your mistakes in life. What he desires is that you simply ask him for his favor. Be favor minded! Seek out opportunities in your day to ask God for his favor upon you. Sometimes I run late in getting home to my husband. A phone call usually takes care of Rocky's concerns. However, this one particular time, my cell phone did not pick up a signal from where I was. Now, Rocky gets very concerned when I am not home at the time he expects. Especially, if I do not confirm with him that there has been a change of plans. Still another forty-five minutes from home, I prayed for God's favor upon me by asking God to give my husband peace over this situation. Then I put my trust in God for answered prayer. I confirmed my trust by singing songs of praise the rest of the way home. That is faith in action. I did not worry about what Rocky might be thinking.

I did not allow my mind to fill up with doubt, worry, or fear of confrontation. I simply sang songs of praise keeping my mind on Jesus the rest of the way home that beautiful sunny afternoon. When I got home, I slowly opened the front door to find my husband sound asleep on the sofa. God knew just what my dear Italian husband needed to stay at peace. I looked up, smiled toward heaven, and whispered, *"thank you Lord."* God wants to bless you to overflowing with his favor. Be favor minded and watch what God will do for you. God can grant you favor upon your finances, your children, your loved ones, at work, anywhere at any time. God's favor is yours. All you have to do is ask him for it. When you believe by faith that you have God's favor, you could ask for a miracle, expecting to receive it. *"Verily I say unto you, if ye have faith, and doubt not, ye shall not only do this which is done to the fig tree, but also if ye shall say unto this mountain, be thou removed, and be thou cast into the sea; it shall be done."* Matthew 21:21. *"for verily I say unto you, if ye have faith as a grain of mustard seed, ye shall say unto this mountain, remove hence to yonder place, and it shall remove; and nothing shall be impossible unto you."* Matthew 17:20.

Faith comes by emptying your mind, your heart, and your life from distractions that lead you away from the things of God. It is about learning to become more God minded and spiritual minded. To understand the things of God, your perspective must change from the natural realm to the supernatural. Transform your mind to become like-minded with God.

Not just during church services but all the time. When you are late for work, the kids are running havoc throughout the house, poor school grades, your teenager is making poor decisions in life, your finances are not what they need to be, sickness, non-supportive spouse the list is endless. Nevertheless, God sees it all and wants you to look beyond the surface of these painful stressful circumstances to the underlying truth of the matter. Ask God to show you how you could be on time for work and your appointments. Seek God for opportunities to help you in the development of your children's hidden talents and abilities, therefore providing them with less time to run amuck throughout the house. Instill into your children good morals and values starting at a young age. Ask God to show you how you could improve your finances. Trust in him for sickness, a supportive spouse, and in all areas of your life one area at a time, step-by-step, prayer-by-prayer. Allow your present circumstances to help you choose to make the necessary changes needed for healthier living. See God as your mediator who already is fully aware of what you are going through. He will not change anything you will not allow him to change. Change begins with you allowing God to work through you from within. Find something good in all situations even when they appear bad. Trust in God for the good and bad days. Be more responsible with your time. Pray for God's favor when you are running late. He is longing to do anything you ask that is right and glorifies him. Remember to ask in complete faith. Instead of asking for the gas prices to go down, pray for God to give you an increase in your paycheck, a promotion, or a better job. Remember Matthew 21:21 previously mentioned and your increase will be greater than increased gas prices. You are God's child. You have his favor upon your life. If your child is not doing well in school, find the thing he does well and encourage him in that area. Poor grades may result from a lack of effort. However, if your child does not feel good about himself in one area, other areas will be affected if he does not have proper support from those closest to him. Encourage your children in the areas they do well. Even in areas that may not be meaningful to you, music, art, library, or gym. Strong areas in your children are gifts from God that need to be nurtured and strengthened through your acceptance and approval. Encouragement in one area helps to motivate your child in other areas. Repeatedly tell your children that you see potential in them; that you see their good side. Building a child's confidence will gradually encourage the need to develop educational skills; *"In all thy ways acknowledge him, and he shall direct thy paths."* Proverbs 3:6. Ask God to *"Create in me* [you] *a clean heart, O God; and renew a right spirit in me* [you]*."* Psalms 51:10. Keep your focus on God. Avoid distractions. Learn to say no to new projects that will only take more of your time away from God. Spend more time in daily devotion to God. Research God's Word. Develop healthy Christian friendships and relationships. Find a good Bible based church for the whole family even if it requires a little traveling to get there. You won't regret it. Be persistent in your prayers. Expect to receive answers. Just remember to fill your mind with the things of God. Be a witness and a light unto others. Daily find ways to bless others and God's blessings will return to you overflowing. You have God's favor when you are God-minded.

You are a new creature in Christ. Old things are done away with. Make room for the new you in Jesus Christ. Miracles do happen every day. Remember, the harvest is plentiful but the laborers are few. Are you willing to be a laborer for God today? Can you let go of your self-image to be molded into the image of God? Will you obey God no matter what others around you may think? Are you truly willing to study the God's Word? Once you begin to let God control your life your reputation with others changes. Your reputation actually gets better because you will be recognized as a man or woman highly favored by God. Your ministry will begin with those around you, at work, home, or in your community. God will watch over you and protect you. *"He will never leave you nor forsake you."* Hebrews 13:5.

Living spirit-minded rather than carnal-minded allows for the expectation of supernatural manifestations from God. Willingly allow God to do what is impossible in the natural. Having the mind of Christ means no longer walking in fear of man. When you trust God in every area of your life, man's image of you will not matter. Take aggressive action towards a life in Christ. Learn to give God your best time. Devote more of your attention to him. Give to God and he will give back to you. Learn to identify his still stall voice, gain wisdom and incite to his Word. He will cause you to prosper, spiritually, physically, and financially. Prepare for the harvest coming your way. It is your time to labor for a blessing. Have God's Word for lunch in the privacy of your car, if necessary. Seek God and you will be blessed. Determine yourself to soar above your circumstances to a life filled with abundance through Jesus Christ. Why, because you are worth it! Allow God to give you wings to soar like an eagle.

*"But they that wait upon the Lord shall renew their strength; they shall mount up with wings as eagles; they shall run, and not be weary; and they shall walk, and not faint."* Isaiah 40:31.

*"The Spirit of the Lord is upon me, because he hath anointed me to preach the gospel to the poor; He hath sent me to heal the brokenhearted, to preach deliverance to the captives, and recovering of sight to the blind, to set at liberty them that are bruised, to preach the acceptable year of our Lord. And he closed the book, and he gave it again to the minister, and sat down. And the eyes of all them that were in the synagogue were fastened on him. And he began to say to them, this day is the scripture fulfilled in your ears."* Luke 4:18-21.

# About the Author

*"I love encouraging people.*
*I always have.*
*I believe in releasing strongholds,*
*Breaking chains of bondage,*
*Embracing the life*
*God truly intended for us to live."*

S usan DeRienzo is a college graduate of Music and the Performing Arts. Her many years as a vocalist, motivational speaker, and children's musical director has won her numerous awards in New York, where she was born. In 1995, Susan won a Tony Award for excellence in creating, producing, and directing musical productions. Susan is also the founder of Harvest Seekers Incorporated, youth and family programs. Having a deep desire to continue reaching out to others with a message of hope inspired Susan to write, How to Soar Like an Eagle.

Pastor Rocky DeRienzo and Associate Pastor Susan DeRienzo, pastor their church together in Perkinston, Mississippi. Associate Pastor Susan also enjoys painting nature scenes and reading. Susan and her husband reside in Kiln, Mississippi.

LaVergne, TN USA
28 August 2010
194940LV00002B/1/P